Supporting Young Childr[en's] Communication Prob[lems]

Now in its fourth edition, formerly published as *How to Manage Communication Problems in Young Children*, this invaluable guide to understanding and helping children whose speech and/or language is delayed or impaired has been completely revised and updated, and provides readers with:

- practical advice on how to recognise communication problems;
- strategies for supporting children with speech, language and communication needs;
- a best practice guide for parents and professionals working in partnership;
- contributions from a wide range of specialist speech and language therapists.

Reflecting new developments and current practice, this book is of interest to parents, early years practitioners, students in education and speech and language therapy, and anyone interested in pursuing a career with young children in the foundation years. Written in an accessible style, it assumes no prior knowledge and includes a range of practical suggestions for dealing with children with all kinds of communication difficulties.

Myra Kersner was previously a Senior Lecturer at University College London, UK.

Jannet A. Wright was formerly Professor of Speech and Language Therapy and Head of the Speech and Language Therapy Division at De Montfort University, Leicester, UK.

Supporting Young Children with Communication Problems

Fourth Edition

Edited by Myra Kersner and
Jannet A. Wright

Routledge
Taylor & Francis Group

LONDON AND NEW YORK

Fourth edition published 2015
by Routledge
2 Park Square, Milton Park, Abingdon, Oxon OX14 4RN

and by Routledge
711 Third Avenue, New York, NY 10017

Routledge is an imprint of the Taylor & Francis Group, an informa business

First edition published by David Fulton Publishers 1996 as *How to Manage
Communication Problems in Young Children*
Third edition published by David Fulton Publishers 2002 as *How to
Manage Communication Problems in Young Children*

British Library Cataloguing-in-Publication Data
A catalogue record for this book is available from the British Library

Library of Congress Cataloging in Publication Data
Supporting young children with communication problems / edited by
Myra Kersner and Jannet A. Wright. -- 4th edition.
pages cm
Revised edition of: How to manage communication problems in young
children.
1. Speech disorders in children. 2. Speech therapy for children. 3.
Language disorders in children. I. Kersner, Myra. II. Wright, Jannet A. III.
Title.
RJ496.S7 H625
618.92'855--dc23
2014042315

ISBN: 978-1-138-77920-4 (hbk)
ISBN: 978-1-138-77921-1 (pbk)
ISBN: 978-1-315-70983-3 (ebk)

Typeset in Sabon
by Saxon Graphics Ltd, Derby

Printed and bound in Great Britain by
TJ International Ltd, Padstow, Cornwall

The fourth edition of this book is dedicated to Renée Byrne, friend, colleague and contributor to previous editions, who died in December 2011.

Contents

Figures

Contributors

Melanie Cross is a consultant speech and language therapist, video interaction guider, clinical tutor, lecturer and trainer. Melanie is also an advisor on child mental health to the Royal College of Speech and Language Therapists and is the author of *Children with Social, Emotional and Behavioural Difficulties and Communication Problems.*

Keena Cummins is a speech and language therapist. She has spent the last twenty-five years learning from and working with parents and children with communication difficulties, through the use of video playback. She has managed an early years service, is a university tutor, has an independent practice and works in early years, primary and secondary schools.

Silke Fricke is a lecturer at the University of Sheffield. As a speech and language therapist she specialised in children with speech, language and literacy difficulties. Since September 2011 she has been involved in various research projects evaluating school-based oral language interventions for monolingual and multilingual children.

Myra Kersner has been a senior lecturer at University College London, where for many years she focussed on students' clinical and professional development. As a speech and language therapist she specialised in working with children and adults with severe learning disabilities. She won an Honours award from the RCSLT. She has co-written many articles and books with Jannet A. Wright, including *Speech and Language Therapy: the decision-making process when working with children.*

Tom Loucas is a speech and language therapist and a lecturer in speech and language pathology at the University of Reading, where he has established a Centre for Autism with colleagues in the School of Psychology and Clinical Language Sciences. His clinical specialism and area of research is autism spectrum disorders.

Alison McLaughlin is an advanced practitioner and a European clinical specialist in fluency disorders with over ten years' experience of working with individuals who stammer and their families. Her experience includes research relating to stammering, raising public and investor awareness of stammering, developing NHS fluency services, delivering highly specialist training nationally and guest lecturing at Manchester University.

Merle Mahon is a senior lecturer in the Developmental Science Research Department, Division of Psychology and Language Science, University College London. Her research focusses on spoken language development in children with hearing impairment, especially those from families where English is an additional language.

Magdalene Moorey is a principal speech and language therapist at Lewisham and Greenwich NHS Trust. She also works as a health commissioner, redesigning services and pathways of care for children with hearing difficulties.

Blanca Schaefer is a speech and language therapist with a special interest in child language acquisition. After working as a post-doctoral research associate in two projects in the UK and holding a professorship in Germany, she is currently working as a visiting lecturer at the University of Chester.

Trudy Stewart is a consultant speech and language therapist and the lead clinician/manager of the Stammering Support Centre, Leeds. She was the first therapist in the UK to gain a PhD in the field of stammering. She has written books, research articles and chapters on many subjects including psychological issues and stammering. She has trained speech and language therapy students in Europe, the USA and Sri Lanka.

Jannet A. Wright was a professor of speech and language therapy and the head of the Speech and Language Therapy Division at De Montfort University, Leicester. She is a Fellow of the RCSLT. She has carried out extensive research into collaboration between speech and language therapists and educational practitioners. She has co-written many articles and books with Myra Kersner, including *A Career in Speech and Language Therapy*.

Preface

Supporting Young Children with Communication Problems is the fourth, revised and completely updated edition of the book *How to Manage Communication Problems in Young Children* that was first published in 1993. The first edition was developed from specialist courses that were run in the Department of Human Communication Science at University College London. These courses, which did not assume prior specialist knowledge, aimed to meet the needs of those who wanted to understand the speech and language problems of young children. However, there were other practitioners and parents who indicated that they wanted to improve their knowledge and learn more about children's difficulties with communication without attending courses. They wanted a book which was 'jargon-free' and accessible.

Contributors who were specialist speech and language therapists with specific expertise and experience with such children were therefore invited to write a chapter about their field of expertise for the original book. Since then, in each new edition some of the chapters have been revised by their original authors, and in this edition, in which new aspects of communication difficulties have been introduced and resources updated, we are pleased to welcome some new specialist contributors.

Learning to talk is something that most children do naturally and without fuss. Helping children to communicate and develop speech and language is something that most adults do spontaneously and without thought. There is no need for us to understand this process, the children's role or the adults' role, no reason to know why, or how, speech and language develops – that is, until something goes wrong. It is not until we come across children who are experiencing difficulties, and who are not learning to talk easily and routinely, that we go in search of knowledge. Then we urgently try to find out more about speech and language development, attempting to discover what has gone wrong and how we might be able to help put it right.

It is not only parents of young children who might find themselves in this situation. Early years workers, nursery nurses, assistants and volunteers as well as teachers of young children may find that they are working with children with speech, language and communication needs (SLCN), and they too welcome information regarding communication problems.

The aim of the book, now entitled *Supporting Young Children with Communication Problems*, is to offer some insight and understanding into some of these difficulties: to indicate what signs to look out for; to offer some interpretation of what these signs might mean; and to suggest how best to help, and where, when and how to seek expert advice. In this fourth edition we have made additions and alterations to reflect new developments and current practice. Increased access to the internet has meant that we have been able to include website addresses for relevant organisations and resources.

We hope that this fourth edition will continue to be a useful text for fellow professionals. It may also be helpful for those who are contemplating a career working with young children by highlighting some of the problems which they may encounter. In addition, we hope that parents will continue to find it a useful resource. We hope that it will help them to understand more fully their children's difficulties, and thus enable all of us to work together for the benefit of the children in our care.

Myra Kersner
Jannet A. Wright
(Editors)

Acknowledgements

We would like to thank Gene Mahon for kindly providing us with the original illustrations for Chapter 3.

We would also like to acknowledge the earlier work of Monica Bray, Rosemarie Morgan Barry, Carolyn Bruce, and our late colleague Sandy Winyard.

Myra Kersner
Jannet A. Wright
(Editors)

Glossary

BLISSYMBOLS: This is a structured system – with its own grammar – of diagrammatic symbols which represent spoken words. The symbol elements are put together in different combinations and are repeated with consistent meaning. It is used most widely by people with physical disabilities to help them to communicate.

BRITISH SIGN LANGUAGE (BSL): The sign language used by many deaf people in Britain. It does not follow the same word order as spoken English, but has a grammar and structure of its own.

CEREBRAL PALSY: Brain damage which may occur before, during or shortly after birth. Children with cerebral palsy usually have some degree of physical disability, which may affect vocal communication. In some cases children may also have learning disabilities.

CLEFT LIP and/or PALATE: A structural abnormality which affects the developing foetus and is present at birth. It involves the hard palate and/or soft palate (roof of the mouth) which fail to meet completely. It may be associated with a cleft lip. Both conditions are normally treated surgically, and treatment may continue until a child is in his/her late teens. In babies and young children there may be feeding difficulties, and some articulation problems may occur.

ENGLISH AS AN ADDITIONAL LANGUAGE (EAL): Refers to children for whom English is not the language spoken in the home. They learn, and often use, English as an additional language.

INTERVENTION: Usually refers to some kind of therapeutic treatment following assessment. This may involve activities, exercises or games that help to minimise a child's speech and language problems and improve their communication skills.

LEARNING DISABILITIES: May also be referred to as learning difficulties, and refers to people who have some degree of cognitive difficulty. In the past it has been referred to as 'mental handicap' or 'mental retardation'.

LOOKED AFTER CHILDREN: The NSPCC defines the term 'looked after children and young people' as being generally used to mean those looked after by the state, according to relevant national legislation. This legislation differs between England, Northern Ireland, Scotland and Wales. The term includes those who are subject to a care order as well as those temporarily classed as 'looked after' on a planned basis for short breaks or respite care.

MAKATON SYMBOLS: A system of stylised pictures which are used to represent the signs of MAKATON. This refers to a system of over three hundred specific signs which have been specially selected from BSL. The symbols are widely used with people with learning disabilities to help them communicate.

ONSET: The initial signs of a communication difficulty, commonly used in relation to stammering.

Please note:

The word 'parents' within the context of this book is used to refer not only to birth or adopted parents but to all those taking on a caring/parental role.

In some chapters the speech and language therapist has been referred to as 'she' and the child as 'he'.

Chapter 1

Speech, language and communication problems in young children

Myra Kersner

The children described in this book are, in the main, the kind of children who may be found in any nursery or classroom. They may have a variety of different types of communication problems. In order to understand these problems it is helpful to understand how communication develops.

Speech, language and **communication** are words which most of us use, comfortably and often, taking for granted that we understand their meaning. However, as with many words, there can be different aspects to their meaning, according to different contexts, and when they are used by speech and language therapists in a professional context they take on a specific meaning. This book has been written by speech and language therapists, and throughout the text these three words are used in their technical sense, in terms of the developing child. It is therefore important that they should be clearly defined at the outset, and that the relationship between them in this context should be explained (see Figure 1.1).

Figure 1.1 illustrates how communication develops as the newborn baby sees, hears and begins to experience the world. Initially the baby communicates using **non-verbal expression** such as crying, laughing or cooing. As the child begins to develop physically, cognitively and emotionally, so the understanding of language develops. This language may then be communicated using **verbal expression** or **speech**. This is more fully developed in Chapter 2.

Communication

Communication is the all-embracing term that includes speech and language but also covers all of the other ways in which we receive and express messages. This might be Morse code, semaphore signals or a sign language, or it might be through text messages, mobile phones, emails, Twitter, Facebook or other forms of social media.

It is generally defined in terms of social interaction – people connecting with each other – and this may occur in many different ways. For example, teenagers who are capable of conducting long telephone conversations or

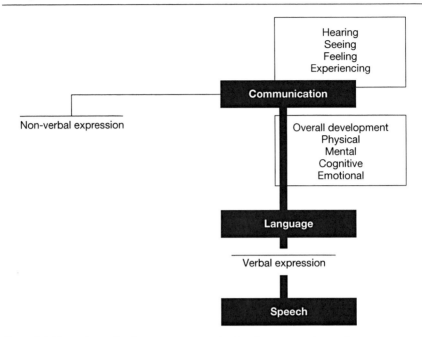

Figure 1.1 The relationship between communication, language and speech

sequences of text messages with their friends often resort to nothing more than a grunt or a shrug when communicating with their parents. Newborn babies who have not yet developed language or speech are also able to communicate, quickly beginning to respond as adults communicate with them (see Chapter 2).

From the first day of life babies receive communication from others, albeit passively, as they begin to see, hear and experience the world around them. When they are held close by a caring adult, when they hear words of comfort, or even angry tones, or when they are merely taking part in the feeding process, they are receiving communication from others.

At the same time, babies are able to communicate actively and express themselves, because from the day they are born they are able to tell us when they are wet, hungry or uncomfortable.

In order to communicate, three basic elements are required: **intention; the means; and a receiver.** This is true even in newborn babies, as illustrated below.

Intention: this refers to the intention to convey a message. For example, babies have the need, almost from the moment of birth, to convey a message expressing their discomfort.

The Means: this is the means by which that message may be conveyed. In young babies, for example, the means to express their discomfort is by crying.

A Receiver: this refers to the person who is required to 'pick up' and respond to the message once it has been sent. With young babies it is usually a parent who hears them crying and is ready to react and respond.

These three elements of communication are usually in place at birth, and it is from this cycle that early **communication patterns** are set (see Figure 1.2).

As Figure 1.2 illustrates, the baby expresses discomfort by crying; the adult carer receives that message and responds, perhaps with soothing words or noises; and the baby hears these noises and responds, perhaps with a modified type of expression such as a whimper or a comfort noise. It is also important to notice that when an adult receives the baby's first message s/he will probably also respond with an action, such as feeding the baby or changing its nappy. This action will reinforce the baby's intention to communicate, because the baby will realise that its attempts to communicate are rewarded by adults' actions.

At first babies are only able to communicate their feelings of discomfort, but gradually they begin to signal 'I am happy; I am comfortable' non-verbally, by cooing, gurgling or smiling, and once again the cycle is reinforced. Normally this repertoire of pre-language, non-verbal forms of expression increases as children develop more understanding of language, until finally they are ready to speak (see Chapter 2).

Language

Although communication begins at birth, language does not develop until the child begins to grow, mature and absorb sensory experiences from the outside world. Language is extremely complex, even though, once acquired, we use it extensively and automatically. Very young babies are motivated to be good communicators and by the time spoken language starts developing, around their first birthday, the basic capacity to use it has begun to develop too.

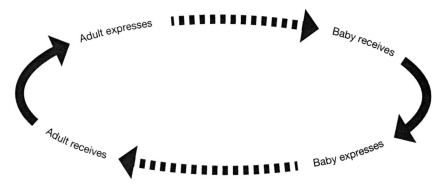

Figure 1.2 Communication patterns

Language is a form of shorthand which is used as a means of classifying and ordering the world. Various symbols are used to represent objects, situations and the everyday occurrences of life. These symbols are the spoken, written or signed words which, over generations, have evolved (and continue to evolve) into an agreed and accepted system of symbols – a particular language. For example, spoken or written English is a system of symbols governed by many hundreds of grammatical rules which are accepted and recognised in this country and by many people throughout the world. Adults may be expected to have about fifty thousand different words which they are able to use, and they will often understand and recognise up to twice that number.

As young children begin to understand the symbols of their own language, gradually they are able to use that language to express their own messages and to improve their communication. It is surprising to realise how many words may be used even by young children. A study cited in Crystal (1986) showed that at seventeen months one child was able to use 1,860 different types of words. These included nouns, naming people and different categories of objects; verbs, describing a variety of actions; descriptive words referring to location; and words such as 'more' and 'again'.

The use of language means that a greater variety of messages may be communicated to larger numbers of people. Language allows messages to be more precisely expressed, so that they will be easily understood. For example, the mother of a fifteen-month-old boy may understand that when he says 'er ber ber' and points his finger he means 'there's a bus over there', but she may be the only person who understands this. However, anyone who understands English will know what he means once he is able to say the words 'look, there's a bus'. By the time the child is five, he may be expected to use over two thousand different words.

Language may be expressed in a variety of ways (see below). Most commonly, however, it is expressed through words which are spoken out loud.

Speech

Speech, or verbal expression, is the mechanism by which most people communicate. Speech requires the use of the voice to make sounds. In English these sounds are then formed and shaped by the tongue, lips, teeth and palate to make twenty vowel sounds and twenty-four consonant sounds, which are then combined in hundreds of different ways to form English words. When these words are heard and understood, the receiver may respond with other words.

Other ways of expressing language

There are other ways in which language may be expressed non-verbally. As Figure 1.3 shows, language may also be expressed using two forms of non-verbal expression: **non-vocal expression** and **body language**.

Non-vocal expression

There are several forms of non-vocal expression. Perhaps the most common is the use of written symbols (letters). This form may be used in books or magazines, or when sending emails or texts. Reading and writing are usually learned after speech has developed, when children go to school.

However, there are some children who may understand language but whose speech does not develop properly. They have to learn to express their language in other ways. This may occur with children who have hearing problems, or with some of those who have learning disabilities; it may be that they have a physical disability, such as cerebral palsy, or they may have a specific problem affecting the speech organs, such as paralysis or a degenerative disease.

In such cases these children may be taught an alternative or augmentative system of communication (AAC) such as a sign language (e.g. British Sign Language), a symbol system where they point to pictures, words or specific symbols (e.g. Makaton Symbols or Blissymbols - see glossary), or they may use written words if they are able to read and write.

In some cases, an AAC might involve the use of a technical aid such as an electronic communication device that may provide an alternative to speech (Clarke et al. 2012).

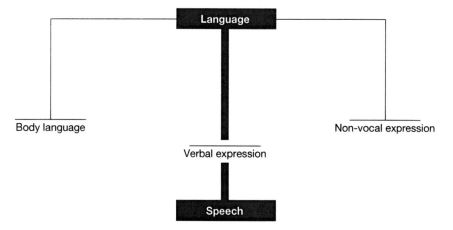

Figure 1.3 Verbal and non-verbal expression

Body language

Body language is another form of non-verbal expression. However, messages communicated through body language, which may be sent either consciously or unconsciously, are usually used in addition to the spoken word. This type of non-verbal expression amplifies speech, giving it another dimension and sometimes even another meaning.

An example of body language is making eye contact, or alternatively avoiding someone's gaze. This gives unspoken messages about the level of confidence, shyness, awkwardness or embarrassment which one may be feeling during a particular interaction. However, it is important to be aware that there may be different uses of eye contact in various cultures.

Stance gives another message. The arms akimbo position with fists on the waist and the elbows pointing outwards is often considered to express aggression, whereas arms folded across the chest may be interpreted as defensive.

Gestures may help to emphasise a spoken message, such as wagging a finger while telling someone off. Gestures may even replace the spoken word, such as when pointing or shrugging the shoulders. Once again it is important to be aware of cultural variations in the use of specific gestures.

Different facial expressions also give additional messages. Smiling or frowning may quickly convey an accurate message regarding feelings, which may help to underline the words of the message.

However, facial expressions may also be used to convey a 'mixed message'. For example, this may occur when a speaker uses an angry voice which is belied by a twinkle of the eye, or when seemingly harmless words are combined with a sarcastic lifting of the eyebrows. Such non-verbal messages play an important role in communication.

Difficulties with communication

Sometimes, however, the ideal relationship between communication, speech and language is not achieved. The links are not made and at some level communication breaks down. In such instances, children may be said to have a 'communication disorder' or speech, language and communication needs (SLCN), which are umbrella terms covering a wide range of difficulties. It is recognised that as many as five per cent of children enter school with some of these difficulties. It would therefore seem to be important for early years workers, teachers and carers to ensure they have an understanding of children's speech and language problems. Indeed, because more children with special educational needs now enter mainstream schools, more education and support staff require knowledge and skills in the management of children with speech and language difficulties.

The relationship between communication, language and speech is a complex one, and the ability to communicate is dependent on the social and emotional as well as the physical environment. It is therefore possible that this ability could break down at any stage during a child's development. The effect this would have on the young child would depend on the level at which the breakdown occurred.

For example, if something went wrong during the early stages of development, before the patterns of communication were fully established, this could result in the child having difficulties in the subsequent development of language, and later in the development of speech. It could interrupt the development of communication patterns with children who have an Autism Spectrum Disorder, for instance (see Chapter 8). On the other hand, if there was a physical problem only affecting the organs of speech, this would not necessarily affect language development or the establishment of communication patterns.

Some children encountered by early years workers within the British health and/or educational system may have developed language normally, but that language may not have been English, so that they will need to learn English as an additional language (EAL). Until they are able to learn to speak English fluently, they may struggle with their speech as they come to grips with new words and different sound combinations. However, this is not the same as a child who struggles because they have SLCN unless that child has difficulties learning the language spoken at home as well as learning English.

Describing children's speech and language

Which terms to use to describe children's abnormal speech and language development is often a point for discussion among speech and language therapists. For example, there is debate, but not always agreement, regarding the use of different terminology. In the following chapters, such words as delayed, disordered, difficulties, problems and impairment are used interchangeably to describe the speech and language of children with SLCN.

While it may not be crucial to differentiate the specific terminology here, it is important to be able to recognise children who have developmental language problems. It is important to be able to broadly classify the area in which they (the children) are having the most difficulty – is it with language? with speech? or with basic patterns of communication? – and to know how to begin to help. If children are not given help the overall result could be that their communicative skills may not be learned at the appropriate time, or may not be learned at all.

The population of children

Children with communication problems may be found in any nursery or mainstream classroom. They may not appear to be different from other children, and yet they may be experiencing some difficulties with speech/language/communication. These are the children who are often in danger of being overlooked, if their particular difficulty is not understood. There are several reasons which might account for their speech and language difficulties, some of which will be dealt with in the following chapters. These include: hearing difficulties; speech and language problems; Autism Spectrum Disorder; social, mental and emotional health problems; and stammering.

Hearing difficulties

Babies are normally able to hear from the moment of birth. If there are difficulties with this fundamental sensory system, it can be seen from Figure 1.1 how the entire communication system and the development of language and speech may be affected to some degree. Some children may enter an early years setting or even begin school with a hearing problem, because the cause of their difficulties has not yet been recognised. Details of how hearing difficulties may affect the young child are described in Chapter 3.

Speech and language problems

Although the diagnosis of specific speech and language disorders requires the specialist knowledge of a speech and language therapist, early years workers and carers are often able to recognise and describe children's communication problems. There is a description and discussion in Chapter 4 of how to recognise and distinguish some of these difficulties.

Stammering

Stammering is a specific problem affecting the speech and language of people of all ages, and as many as five per cent of the population may have stammered at some time in their lives. Although fewer children are affected by stammering than by other disorders, stammering may sometimes prove more difficult to manage than other speech problems. Stammering affects verbal expression, which may sound as if it is 'broken up' and not fluent. The problems which may arise with children who stammer, and how they may be helped, are dealt with in Chapter 6.

Social, mental and emotional health problems

Although emotional difficulties may arise as a result of speech and language problems, and the resultant frustration of having an impaired communication system, it can be seen from Figure 1.1 that emotional development plays an important role in the growth and progress of the child as a whole, and particularly in the development of language and speech. Some social, mental and emotional health difficulties may also contribute to communication and/or language problems. This is discussed more fully in Chapter 7.

Autism Spectrum Disorders (ASD)

ASD is a common difficulty in childhood which affects the development of speech, language and social interaction, and it is now well documented that children who have ASD will experience some form of SLCN. The exact causes are unknown, and diagnosis relies on the expertise and experience of the members of the Autism Team working with the child. However, there are several different approaches to intervention, and the ways in which support may be offered to the child and their family are dealt with in Chapter 8.

How can you help?

The development of language and speech is an intrinsic and integral part of the development of the child as a whole, and there are many ways in which children can be helped if they are experiencing difficulties with this aspect of their development, as discussed in Chapters 9 and 10. Chapter 9 focusses on how language development may be enhanced by the use of formal language programmes. However, there are also many games and activities which are useful for such children which teachers could incorporate into their curriculum planning, or which early years workers and/or parents could incorporate into the child's routine within the nursery or at home. Ideas and suggestions for the inclusion of these informal activities are given in Chapter 10.

Working with parents

It is acknowledged that parents are often among the first to recognise that something is wrong with their child, and it is therefore important for them to be included in the helping process whenever possible. How professionals may collaborate with parents in order to facilitate this aspect of their work is discussed in Chapter 5.

Of course, there are many other groups of children who have speech and language difficulties which are beyond the scope of this book. Mostly these are children who have communication disorders as a result of physical problems such as cerebral palsy, or children with severe or mild learning disabilities. Many of these children may need specific specialist help. However, there are many children with SLCN who can be helped by a speech and language therapist, particularly if s/he is able to work collaboratively with parents, teachers and early years workers.

The speech and language therapist

Wherever possible it is best to seek the advice of a speech and language therapist, to discuss the ways in which to help any child with a communication difficulty.

Speech and language therapists are the professionals to contact if a child is known to have a speech and language problem, or if professional education/care workers or parents are concerned about the way in which a child communicates (RCSLT 2006).

In the UK most speech and language therapists are employed by the National Health Service, although many may work in early years settings as well as schools. As discussed above, communication begins at birth, so therapists may become involved with children and their families very early in a child's development. This may be to help not only with communication but also if there are any feeding problems, such as those associated with a cleft lip and/or palate, or a physical problem that has been identified at birth. For further description and discussion about cleft lip and palate, see Sell and Harding-Bell (2012).

A therapist evaluates children's speech and language in order to establish their communicative abilities. Each child will be looked at individually. The therapist will also try to consider patterns of interaction, i.e. how the child relates to people in their home environment, in order to establish whether there are any particular features which may be contributing to the communication difficulties. With the parents' permission, the therapist will also talk to the child's early years workers or teachers about how the child communicates with staff and other children. The therapist may be able to work with the teachers and the parents to help the child, integrating such things as curriculum topics and the school's teaching methods into the therapy. Increasingly therapists may help the parents or early years practitioners to work with the children themselves.

Service delivery

The local arrangements for speech and language therapy service provision will vary from one geographical area to another. Thus, for example, in Yorkshire a child with a communication problem, and those working with that child, will find services are organised in a different way from those provided for children with the same problems in Cornwall.

The way in which therapists work may also vary. In some areas therapists will work directly with the children, while in other areas therapists work 'indirectly', training others to continue therapy with the children.

Health centre services

Even within one geographical area speech and language therapists may vary the frequency of the appointments that they offer. This will depend on the needs of the child, the family's commitments, the therapist's rationale for the management of that child, and the policy and organisation of the local services. The length of time that children and their families spend with a therapist will vary, depending on the needs of the children. Sometimes an appointment will last thirty to forty-five minutes, whereas some appointments may last up to one and a half hours.

Children may be seen as part of a group, in which case parents may be asked to bring their child for a whole morning or an afternoon. Parents may then be expected to continue to work with the child regularly at home until the next appointment. Parents need to be involved as much as possible from the time of referral.

Education-based services

In an increasing number of areas speech and language therapists are working within early years settings and schools as well as special schools, where they liaise directly with early years workers, teachers and assistants. The teachers and the therapist will discuss the effect of the communication problem on the child's academic work. They will also decide how therapy may be integrated into curricular activities, and how relevant new vocabulary and topics may be incorporated into the therapy. Sometimes therapists may work with an individual child or a group of children within the classroom. Often, regular therapy may be continued by an assistant whom the therapist has trained.

What will the speech and language therapist do?

The speech and language therapist needs to obtain a complete picture of the child, including speech and language skills. The assessment of communication problems involves using materials with which children are comfortable, namely toys and books. The way in which they play can reveal a great deal about the way in which they think and understand the world around them, and aspects of their intellectual functioning. The therapist will also be interested in the children's attention span and their ability to concentrate – for example, noting how long they play with one toy or one game. They will also observe their interaction skills and their non-verbal communication such as gestures, pointing and eye contact.

The therapist will need to assess the child and take a full case history from the parent, and establish whether the child's problems are related to any hearing difficulties.

The therapist will try to work out how much a child understands, using a variety of assessment techniques. It may appear that children 'understand everything that is said to them', but this may not be the case.

The therapist will take a language sample which they can then analyse and compare to developmental norms to identify a child's communication strengths and weaknesses. The therapist will note the grammatical structures as well as the vocabulary the child uses.

They also listen to the speech sounds the children use in single words as well as in continuous speech, to see if there is a pattern in the way certain sounds are produced, omitted or substituted. Therapists will also look at how the child interacts with their parents and siblings as this helps them to assess and understand the full range of the child's communicative abilities.

Speech and language therapy sessions will only be successful if the therapy is then incorporated into a child's lifestyle. If speech and language therapy is offered in an educational setting the therapist will have to make decisions about whether to see the child in the classroom or take them out into another room for individual therapy. Close collaboration between the therapist, all other professionals and the parents is necessary if a child is to receive a coordinated programme of intervention which will enable them to integrate their newly acquired skills into their everyday lives.

References

Clarke, M., Price, K. and Jolleff, N. (2012) Augmentative and Alternative Communication. In M. Kersner and J.A. Wright (eds) (2nd edition), *Speech and Language Therapy: the decision-making process when working with children.* London: Routledge.

Crystal, D. (1986) *Listen to your Child: Parents' guide to children's language.* Harmondsworth: Penguin Books.

Royal College of Speech and Language Therapists (2006) *Communicating Quality 3.* London: RCSLT.

Sell, D. and Harding-Bell, A. (2012) Cleft Palate and Velopharyngeal Anomalies. In M. Kersner and J.A. Wright (eds) (2nd edition), *Speech and Language Therapy: the decision-making process when working with children.* London: Routledge.

Further reading

Crystal, D. (2007) *How Language Works: How babies babble, words change meaning, and languages live and die.* London: Penguin.

Wright, J.A. and Kersner, M. (2013) (3rd edition) *A Career in Speech and Language Therapy.* London: Metacom Education.

Chapter 2

The development of communication

Speech and language acquisition

Myra Kersner

As discussed in Chapter 1, the process of communicating starts from birth, and the development of communication into language and speech begins as the newborn baby draws its first breath.

Communication is an **interactive process**; that means that more than one person is involved. Even from birth it is something that does not occur alone – it is dependent on other factors, such as people and events. This can be illustrated by thinking about any conversation. What one person says is dependent on what the other person says, on their reactions to the first person's communication. In most instances the first people to communicate with the newborn are the parents, and their role in facilitating and encouraging continuing speech, language and communication development is critical as the child grows and develops.

Communication is both verbal and non-verbal. The verbal part of communication is the words that are spoken. The non-verbal part consists of facial expression, such as smiling and frowning, eye contact, and gestures such as beckoning, pointing or waving. Body language also provides non-verbal information for the listener. For example, slouching and turning away from someone indicates disinterest and boredom, while sitting up straight and turning towards someone indicates interest and attention. Normally communication requires both verbal and non-verbal skills, and it is important to remember that much information is conveyed by both methods.

Language development

Language can be divided into **expression** and **comprehension**. Expression is what people say or do that conveys what they want to communicate. Comprehension is what people understand from verbal messages when they are spoken to, and what they understand from what is conveyed in a non-verbal way by gestures and/or body language.

Language can be described by breaking it down into several parts.

Sounds

The sounds in spoken English do not match the letters of the alphabet in written English. For example:

- the letter 'a' is pronounced differently in the words 'pan', 'pane' and 'park';
- the 'sh' sound in words like 'shop' and 'shape', although it is said as one sound, is written with two letters from the alphabet;
- CAT is written with three letters and has three sounds C-A-T, but SHARP has five letters and three sounds SH-AR-P.

When children are learning to talk, it is the sounds that are learned, not the letters. It is these sounds that they sometimes have problems with during their development (see Chapter 4).

Content

This is the words or **vocabulary** which make up the meaning of a message; that is, what children want to convey. Children may sometimes try to convey the same message as an adult, but the way that they say it may sound different. Child language is different from adult language. It is not incorrect or wrong; rather, it is developing.

Some children may pronounce the words incorrectly. For example, they may confuse some sounds in words, so that they say 'tat' instead of 'cat' or 'gog' instead of 'dog'.

Their sentences may be incomplete. For example: 'Daddy sock' may mean 'Daddy, I want my sock', or 'This is Daddy's sock'. Or it could mean, 'Daddy, this is my sock'.

The order of the words may be incorrect. For example, a child may say 'Go car me' instead of 'Me go car', meaning 'I want to go in the car'.

However, despite sounding different, the message may still be clear to the listener because **contextual clues** may be given; that is, information within the context which will help the understanding of the message. This may come from the general situation, or from previous knowledge and information which is known to the two people who are communicating.

For example, Jack asks his mother, 'Where loon?' What he means is, 'Where is the balloon?'

His mother's interpretation of this is dependent on her knowledge of his language as well as her knowledge of her child and his environment. His mother may know that he has been playing with a balloon, or that he has called it a 'loon' previously, or else she may have been told about it by someone who has seen the balloon game. Because she has this information, the mother can understand what Jack is talking about.

Grammar – Syntax

Grammar refers to the rules of language and is sometimes referred to as syntax. The words which express ideas, give information and convey feelings are not put together in a haphazard way. They are organised into structured sentences according to the grammatical rules of the specific language.

For example, when describing the size and colour of an object in English, size always comes before colour. Thus we say a 'big blue ball', not a 'blue big ball'.

In summary, language comprises sounds, which combine to make words, which combine to make sentences.

Use

Language fulfils a variety of communication functions such as greeting people, asking questions, explaining a problem or telling a story. The **use** of language, or **pragmatics**, refers to the way language, both verbal and non-verbal, is used appropriately in different social situations. For example, children use language in a more informal way when talking to their friends than when talking to their teachers. The majority of children learn spontaneously how to use language appropriately. For example, they learn how to take turns in conversations, how to start a conversation, how to end it, how to keep it going, how to correct an error and 'repair' it should they make a mistake, and how to change the topic in an appropriate way.

Intonation

This means the rising or falling sound patterns of speech, or the melody. Intonation has an important role in communication because it is this melody which is one of the first features of speech and language that children both understand and produce. The intonation carries much of the information about the content or meaning of a message.

For example, if the sentence 'We're going out' is said as a statement, announcing the intention to go out, the intonation usually goes down so that the voice will drop at the end. Try saying it.

The same sentence can be turned into a question by changing the intonation pattern. For a question, the intonation rises at the end. Now try saying 'We're going out?' as a question. Can you hear the difference?

Young children rely on the information provided by intonation patterns to help them understand what is said, long before they understand the individual words in a sentence they hear.

Voice

Voice is produced when yelling, shouting or speaking. The air which is breathed in is forced out of the lungs through the mouth and/or nose. This stream of air passes through the vocal cords or vocal folds which are situated in the neck. Try putting a finger on your Adam's apple, the lump of cartilage on the front of your neck. The vocal cords or **larynx** are within this protuberance. Say 'bbb'. You will feel vibrations. This is because the vocal cords are vibrating as the air passes through them.

Children frequently use a loud voice, and at school they often shout in the playground. It is possible for their voices to become hoarse because of excessive shouting. If hoarseness persists, then they may need to be seen by a speech and language therapist to help them use their voices less stridently.

The same can happen to adults, especially teachers who have to project their voices over a noisy classroom. They may strain their voices and become hoarse. They may even 'lose' their voice. If this happens, they too may need help from a speech and language therapist, or from a doctor, or an Ear, Nose and Throat (ENT) Specialist.

How do children learn language?

Imitation

If asked how children learn language, some people would say it was by imitation – they hear words and copy them. There is no doubt that some of the words children produce are imitated. For example, three-year-old Sam was overheard saying to his best friend, 'You can't have ice cream until you've eaten your dinner.' He used exactly the same words, as well as the voice and intonation pattern, that his mother used to him a few days earlier. This is a clear example of imitation.

However, imitation cannot tell the whole story about how children learn to speak. Even allowing for the fact that children hear many different examples of language, from many different sources, such as at home, with friends or at school, imitation cannot account for the new and original ways in which children then produce and use language themselves.

If children learned to speak only by imitation we would expect children's speech to be the same as adults' speech. However, as we saw before, the language of the child is not a replica of the language of an adult – it is different. It seems to have its own patterns and to follow its own rules.

No matter how often you say 'Daddy has just gone to work in the car', children can only attempt to repeat such a sentence using the language that corresponds to the level or stage of their development. For example, in the case of two-and-a-half-year-old Ben, his attempted repetition of this sentence was 'Daddy go work car.'

Another way children's speech differs from adults' speech is that children do not indulge in 'babytalk' in the way that adults do. For example, how many children refer to their toes as 'piggy wiggies'?

Another argument against imitation is that, by adult standards, children's language is full of errors. For example, children talk about 'mouses' – they do not immediately imitate the word 'mice'. Similarly they use 'goed' instead of 'went' and 'badder' instead of 'worse'. This is quite normal – all children go through these stages while they are developing language. The rate at which they develop may vary, with some taking longer than others to progress through the stages of 'child language' to mature language structures.

Innate ability

If imitation does not explain how language develops, then how do children develop language? There are a significant number of researchers in this area, such the prestigious academic Noam Chomsky, who feel that children are born with an innate ability to produce language. The language they are exposed to in their environment, which they hear all around them, then triggers this inbuilt ability.

This theory certainly offers an explanation as to how children are able to learn a limited number of words and use them in combinations which they have obviously never heard before.

These two approaches focus on the child rather than the people who communicate or interact with the child, whereas the interaction approach outlined below focusses on the way that adults and children communicate together.

Adult–child interaction and the development of language

This approach focusses on the person in conversation with the child – for example, the mother – who is thought to be important in the development of language. Work on this approach was based on original research by Bruner (1975). Here, the mother's contribution or **input** is thought to be fundamental to the child's normal development of speech and language.

Viewed from the perspective of the child, language development in terms of adult–child interaction may be considered in two stages – pre-verbal and verbal.

Pre-verbal stage

The pre-verbal stage covers the period from babies' first cries to the emergence of their first words. The adults' input during this stage is important because initially it is the way that adults respond to the cries and physical actions of babies that gives those cries and actions meaning. A baby who wriggles, kicks and cries could be trying to communicate:

'I'm hungry'
'I'm uncomfortable and wet and want to be changed'
'I want to be picked up and made a fuss of'

The adult interprets the meaning by responding to the baby's behaviour, for example by offering food, changing a dirty nappy or picking up and cuddling the infant. The way the adult responds will influence the child's behaviour.

In this way children learn that some of their messages mean something to the adults around them, and that some of their messages are ignored and need to be altered before the adults will respond in the required way.

Of course, this can be a two-way process, and sensitive adults learn from the babies' responses whether they have responded appropriately to the messages.

During this pre-verbal stage babies spend a great deal of time practising the sounds and melodies of speech. They will make noises, and their mothers will often make the same noises back. This is one of the ways in which babies learn the **turn-taking skills** which are required for later stages in their language development, when they need to learn how to use language in social contexts and to take turns in verbal conversations.

Listening and attention

In order to interact in this way young children have to be able to listen and pay attention, and long before they can talk they will listen and attend when an adult is talking. Listening and attending is more than just hearing, more than just being aware of noises and happenings all around; it involves actively concentrating on the noises in the environment. Babies demonstrate that they are really listening by focussing on the adult's face and stopping all activity while the adult is talking. When the adult stops talking they start to make noises and thrash around with their limbs as they 'take their turn' in the conversation (see Chapter 5).

By about nine months children realise that they can influence adult behaviour by using various communication strategies like gestures, vocalisations, or even by making eye contact. This may be considered to be intentional behaviour because children really want the particular message they are sending to be understood. They know what they are trying to communicate and they are sending signals using the same combination of sounds, gestures or looks which in the past have achieved the responses they want from the adult.

For example, baby Fadila, at eleven months, knows that the sounds 'erer', said with a certain intonation together with a pointing gesture, will always result in her getting a drink. Therefore she will reproduce it next time she wants a drink.

Child-directed speech

When interacting with young babies, adults or older children employ a different sort of communication style. This child-directed speech tends to be simpler than the speech used when talking to an adult, and while the sentences are correct in grammar and sounds, they tend to be short and simple in their construction. Speech is often slower, louder and on a higher note, and words which the adult really wants the child to understand are emphasised by putting more stress on them. For example, 'Owen, go and get the ball, get the *ball*.'

Vocal play

While building turn-taking skills with their mothers, babies still have time for practising their speech by playing with sounds. They progress from crying and making basic sounds through happy, cooing noises, to vocal play. Vocal play is quite melodic and babies often bang toys in time with their vocalisations. This stage is reached at about four months.

For example, Sarita was four months old when she began to produce a greater variety of sounds – vowel sounds like 'ah', 'oo' and 'oh' and consonant sounds like 'g', 'k' and 'm' became common. She produced one sound and then repeated it over and over again. She also produced trills and blew 'raspberries'. All of these are common features at this age, and are typical of vocal play.

Babbling

At about six months the babbling stage begins. Most people are familiar with this and remember the long strings of 'babababababa' or 'dadadadada' sounds which infants produce. As the baby continues to babble the sounds become more varied and change within the string, so that strings like 'madumadu' may be produced.

Jargon

At about nine months the intonation patterns of speech are picked up more intensely and practised. Gradually the length of sounds children produce increases, and they sound as if they are producing adult speech. In fact they are not using real words, they are producing strings of sounds with intonation patterns they have learnt from adults. This is called jargon.

By the end of this phase, children are ready to enter the verbal stage. They have acquired many **functional communication skills**: they have learnt the conversational skills of turn-taking, listening and attending; they have practised using their voice, different intonation patterns and sounds; and they have practised using some content, and getting their message across to their listener. They continue to practise these functional communication skills, by making their needs known and manipulating their world by intentionally communicating. They have begun to realise the power of language and they have not yet said a word!

Verbal stage

Into this non-verbal framework of sounds and intonation, at about twelve to fifteen months the child begins to insert words. The first words children say are usually the names of things that are important to them in their personal world. The first words might be 'cup', 'bear', 'car', 'drink', names of the family, or pets. These words may not be pronounced perfectly; for example, cup might be 'cu' or drink might be 'dint' or 'dink'. However, by this stage the word is always used to mean the same thing, showing that the child has attached meaning to it and is using it consistently to convey the same message.

Generalisation

Sometimes children use the same word to mean a number of things that seem similar to them. So, for a period in the child's language development the word 'dog' might be used for all the four-legged animals the child comes across, such as dogs, cats and horses.

A common example of this **generalisation** is the use of the word 'Daddy' or 'Mummy'. Once learnt, 'Daddy' may then be used for all men, and 'Mummy' for all women. A similar process may also happen with the name of the family pet. It is very common to hear a child calling everybody's cat 'Smokey' because that is the name of their own cat. Gradually children learn to refine these umbrella terms or generalisations, learning, for example, that a cat is different from a dog. They also learn that not all men are Daddy.

The 'two-word' stage

A little later in their development – from approximately two years upwards – children begin to put two words together. These two-word phrases or sentences are the beginnings of real grammar and may represent a number of different functions such as statements, requests and questions.

For example:

'Car gone' is a statement meaning 'The car has gone.'
'Mummy biscuit?' is a request meaning 'Mummy, please may I have a biscuit?'

'Where train?' – spoken with a rising inflection – is a question meaning 'Where is the train?' or 'Where has the train gone?'

These are examples of how children are able to get their message across successfully to their listeners using a restricted and immature grammar or rule system, and knowing only a small number of words.

How the listener interprets the meaning of the child's language is important. For example, when two-year-old Alicja says a phrase like 'Mummy shoe', she might mean:

'Mummy, where's my shoe?' (a question);
or 'Mummy, where's your shoe?' (a question);
or 'Mummy, here's your shoe' (a statement);
or 'Mummy, here's my shoe' (a statement).

The intonation pattern will reveal whether she meant the words to be a question or a statement. However, whether she meant it to refer to her mother's shoe or her own shoe will be revealed by contextual clues, such as the general situation, or by other language that has been used before or after the phrase in question.

A child may want to convey a number of different messages using the same two words, and it is only by understanding the situation and listening to the intonation pattern that the listener can make the correct interpretation. This illustrates how the listener helps the child to expand his/her language skills. The listener does this by understanding the message the child is trying to communicate, as well as by using other clues such as the intonation pattern, the environment and any gestures which the child may use to help communication. The listener shows that they have understood by responding appropriately.

Acknowledging, reinforcing, modelling and expanding

Adults help children to develop their language skills by acknowledging that they have said something, reinforcing what they have said, and modelling a correct or mature response. They may also expand what children have said, providing more information about the subject, so that children's vocabulary and knowledge of the language grows.

For example, Katherine, aged two-and-a-half, and her mother are out shopping in the high street one day. Katherine suddenly says, 'Mummy, bu', pointing at a bus. Her mother replies appropriately: 'Yes, it's a bus' (reinforcing/recasting and modelling). She then expands: 'A big, red bus with people on. We could go on a bus to see granny tomorrow. Would you like that?'

Katherine's mother has provided acknowledgement, by saying 'Yes'. She has reinforced/recast and provided the correct model, by repeating what

Katherine has said but using the adult form – 'bus' instead of 'bu'; and she has expanded what Katherine said by telling her more about it. This will encourage Katherine to keep the conversation going, because her mother showed interest in what she was talking about. Her mother did not introduce a new subject; she followed Katherine's lead by talking about her choice of subject. If she is responded to in this way, Katherine should feel good about communicating and hopefully will continue to do so.

These strategies can be particularly useful if children are having difficulty learning to talk. Then the adults around them have to become aware of strategies which they may have used previously, unconsciously, and try to use them intentionally in order to encourage language development.

If you think about how you communicate with children, you probably do this quite naturally most of the time. Try and be aware of the messages you are giving to the children you talk to. Are you encouraging, like Katherine's mother in the example above? Or could your messages sound discouraging? For example, this could be conveyed by not acknowledging what the child has said, or by changing the subject to one of your own choice.

As long ago as 1985, Gordon Wells suggested that children practise language skills with children of their own age, but learn language from people who are older and who are skilled language users themselves.

Concept Development

At the same time as language is developing, young children are developing concepts. These help children to put some order into their world and to understand the world around them. Concept development may be reflected in their use of language, although the stages of development of concepts and language do not always coincide.

Possession

Once the child understands the concept of possession the word 'mine' may be used a great deal, although not always appropriately – such as in 'Mine teddy', 'Mine cup'. The word 'yours' may be used, but again probably inappropriately at first, because the concept of sharing one's possessions with someone else is not yet understood.

Position

Similarly, when children begin to use words which indicate position, for example 'in', 'on', 'under', the ability to use such words correctly is linked to their intellectual development. Children will begin to use the words in phrases such as 'doll in chair', 'cup on table' long before they have understood that 'in', 'on' or 'under' refer to a specific position.

Size, shape, colour

The words indicating the size, shape or colour of an object may be used at first in imitation, without any real understanding of what they mean. As children begin to learn the concept of size and shape, they may begin to use the words appropriately — for example, 'Dat big cup', 'My big bed'. As they understand the concept of comparison they will begin to acknowledge the difference between a big bed and small bed, and they will need to understand the concept of possession before they can use the words 'my bed' and 'your bed'. Between their third and fourth birthdays they will begin to recognise and name colours, as in 'Where's the yellow ball?'

The understanding and use of position words and vocabulary to describe size and colour gives children a more precise grasp of language. When asking for a special cup from the top shelf in the kitchen they can now say 'Red one', which is much quicker and more efficient than saying 'dat one' and pointing. Although previously the message would have been understood, it might have taken longer to convey the same information, depending on the number of choices available. Children quickly learn how useful it is to be more precise with language, and may well practise their new skills by demanding all sorts of things.

Adults also enjoy children's growing language skills as it means they no longer have to spend as much time working out the meaning of what children are saying. Communication is quicker and more fun, and parents are often delighted to tell others of the new vocabulary that is being used all the time. As children are more involved in tasks in the home and actually experience activities such as washing up, dusting, making the beds and fixing broken objects they will talk about them at the same time. This gives them the best possible experience of language at its most meaningful.

The development of grammatical structure

By their third year children are quite sophisticated language users, able to make statements and describe things, ask questions and claim possession appropriately. The third year is often thought of as the one when the most linguistic progress occurs, although to the adult listener the child's speech is full of grammatical errors. For example, word endings are often incorrect.

Tenses

When trying to form the past tense of a regular verb such as 'walk', 'jump' or 'want', children work out that there is a rule about adding '-ed'. They will then over-generalise this new rule by adding '-ed' to all verbs, even irregular ones where this rule does not apply, producing sentences like:

'I goed' or 'I wented' instead of 'I went';
'I runned' instead of 'I ran';
'I eated' instead of 'I ate'.

The future tense which is regularly formed by adding 'will', as in 'I will come', 'I will jump', does not appear in their speech until children develop the concept of future time.

Plurals

The same mistakes will occur as with past tenses, when children need to form the plural of nouns. They learn the regular rule that if they are referring to more than one object they need to add an 's', such as 'bed/beds'.

However, this does not work for irregular nouns like mouse (plural: mice), sheep (sheep) or foot (feet). In an attempt to apply the newly learned rule children will often produce the words 'mouses', 'sheeps' and 'feets'. Gradually they learn the correct form. This is partly achieved by adults responding in the way previously described – that is, by giving the correct and accepted model of the word while reinforcing the use of the meaning.

Questions

In the early stages of language development, questions are asked using a rising intonation pattern – for example, 'Me going out?', 'Daddy go work?' Then children learn that specific question words such as 'Where?', 'What?', 'Why?', 'When?' and 'How?' get both adult attention and information, and they begin to use these words often. Such questions can be a cause of great embarrassment to adults, as they are not always used in the appropriate time and place. This is a great delight to children, often encouraging them to do it again. This is demonstrated in the following example.

On a crowded bus, Lucy, aged three, asks in a loud voice about the young girl sitting two seats in front: 'Mummy, why has that lady got pink hair?' Observing the reaction from her mother and everyone else on the bus, Lucy is encouraged to repeat it. The response from using question words, including the reaction as well as the information gained, means that children will use them frequently.

The third year is often described as the 'why' stage, as this is the age at which children frequently use the word 'why' – not always appropriately.

Word order

Children are learning and absorbing so much new information about their environment and language that they sometimes get their words in the wrong order. For example, they may say sentences like 'They looked at very funny faces with each other' instead of 'They looked at each other with very funny faces'. It is usually when children are trying out new constructions that they make errors. However, even when making errors, children usually succeed in getting their message across correctly.

As children begin to have more to say, they want to talk in longer and more complex sentences. At first they cope with this by linking several short sentences together using the word 'and' – for example, 'And we're going there and teddy and I want dolly and that doll and that one and Rupert Bear.'

Gradually other words such as 'like', 'but', 'because', 'so' and 'or' are introduced. They enable children to use complex sentences containing more than one idea, linking the ideas together – for example, 'Can we go to the beach, because I want to swim?' or 'I want to go out, but it's raining.'

Conclusion

The normal development of language and communication skills shows a great deal of variation and some children may continue to make grammatical errors until ten years or sometimes even later. The development and expansion of children's language skills continues, going hand in hand with their growing experience.

References

Bruner, J.S. (1975) The Ontogenesis of Speech Acts *Journal of Child Language*, 2 (1), 1-20.
Wells, G. (1985) *Language Learning and Education*. Windsor: NFER Nelson.

Further reading

Coupe O'Kane, J. and Goldbart, J. (2000) *Communication Before Speech*. London: David Fulton Publishers.
Lathey, N. and Blake, T. (2013) *Small Talk: Simple ways to boost your child's speech and language development from birth*. London: Macmillan.

Chapter 3

Recognising hearing problems

Magdalene Moorey and Merle Mahon

This chapter describes what is meant by hearing loss, discusses the effects of a hearing loss on speech, language and communication development, and considers ways in which problems may be identified and managed.

What is meant by hearing loss?

Hearing ability is usually measured in terms of the quietest sounds that can be detected across a range of frequencies (**pitches** or **tones**). 'Normal' hearing is described as the quietest sounds which can be heard by a young healthy adult. This is called the normal threshold of hearing. When sounds have to be made louder before a person can detect them, this is described as a raised threshold of hearing, meaning that the person has a hearing loss. Hearing loss can range in severity from mild to profound or total, and can affect some frequencies more than others. Some types of hearing loss are temporary, such as hearing loss caused by middle ear problems (these are usually called temporary fluctuating conductive hearing losses), while other types are permanent and remain throughout life (these are usually called sensorineural hearing losses). Children with sensorineural hearing loss are referred to as having permanent childhood hearing impairment or PCHI. In this chapter we will cover both temporary hearing loss and PCHI.

There are many causes of hearing loss, although sometimes the underlying cause cannot be identified. Some possible causes include:

- inherited disorders and genetic syndromes;
- damage to the hearing mechanism resulting from problems during pregnancy;
- medication given for potentially life-threatening illnesses such as meningitis;
- diseases of the ear;
- extended exposure to loud noises;
- in adults, hearing loss can be associated with ageing.

The hearing mechanism

The hearing mechanism (see Figure 3.1) can be divided into two main parts:
1. the conductive system comprising the outer ear, the ear canal and the middle ear; and 2. the sensorineural system comprising the inner ear (the cochlea) and the auditory nerve. It may help to think of the outer and middle ears as part of a mechanical system of levers, drums and moving parts which work together to conduct sounds to the inner ear. The inner ear is a sensory system (the cochlea) that converts sound into bio-electrical signals, coupled with a neural system (the auditory nerve) that then takes these signals to the brain.

Damage to the hearing mechanism

The location and extent of any damage to the hearing mechanism will affect the nature and degree of any hearing loss. Any damage or disruption to the outer and middle ears will reduce the ear's capacity to conduct sounds to the inner ear. This sort of damage is therefore said to give rise to conductive hearing loss, which is usually temporary. Sounds seem 'muffled' and complex sounds such as speech may become difficult to hear, with the quieter speech sounds like 'f', 's', 'sh' and 'p' becoming inaudible.

Making speech louder often helps to overcome a temporary conductive hearing loss. There are also medical and surgical procedures that can help

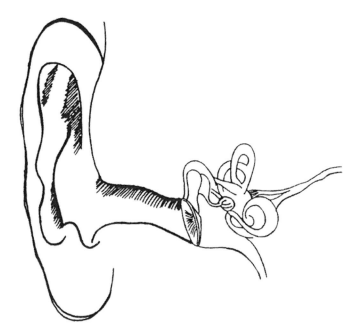

Figure 3.1 Outer, middle and inner ear

alleviate the problem. However, these problems can be short-lived and may resolve without the need for intervention.

Damage to the cochlea and the auditory nerve in the inner ear results in a permanent **sensorineural hearing loss**. In children this is called permanent childhood hearing impairment or PCHI. PCHI can range in severity from mild to profound or total loss. Hearing for different frequencies can be differently affected: generally, high frequencies are more often affected than low. This results in speech sounding not only quieter, but also distorted. A useful comparison is when a battery-operated radio is beginning to run down. Speech becomes fuzzy and indistinct; turning up the volume may make the speech louder, but it does not make it easier to understand what is being said.

There are currently no medical or surgical interventions for treating sensorineural hearing loss, although there is much research in this area. Treatment is focussed on making use of the hearing that remains via the amplification of sound using a hearing aid or a cochlear implant.

PCHI in young children is still relatively rare in the UK. Studies consistently report an incidence of one per every thousand births. Consequently, an early years worker or teacher may only meet one or two infants with PCHI in their career. In contrast, conductive hearing loss is extremely common in young children: approximately seventy per cent of children have experienced at least one episode of glue ear by their third birthday. Although less severe in its impact than PCHI, this is a problem that most carers or educators of young children will encounter.

Middle ear problems resulting in temporary conductive hearing loss

Middle ear problems are very common in young children, who may have one or more episodes in the first years of life. These conditions are collectively known as **Otitis Media** (otitis means 'of the ear'; media means 'the middle') and they are much more common in children than in adults. This is because the horizontal angle of the Eustachian tube in children makes it more likely that blockages will occur (see Figure 3.2). Otitis Media is also thought to be related to children's relatively immature mechanisms for fighting infection. Otitis Media is more common in some children in the winter months if they get colds, and in others in the summer if they have allergies. Certain groups of children are more prone to developing Otitis Media, such as children with Down's syndrome or a cleft palate, and children with a low birth weight.

The most common type of Otitis Media is often called 'glue ear'. In the early stages the condition is called Acute Otitis Media (AOM): the passage that connects the middle ear to the nose, the **Eustachian tube**, may become blocked. The supply of air needed to keep the middle ear cavity healthy is not refreshed and within weeks the cavity can become full of fluid. In this

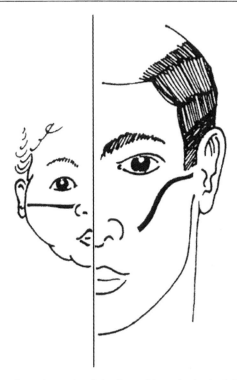

Figure 3.2 Diagram to show the angle of the Eustachian tube in the infant and the adult

state the middle ear is significantly less effective in conducting sound to the inner ear. If the Eustachian tube remains blocked, the fluid in the middle ear thickens over time and after a number of weeks may have the consistency of glue, hence the familiar label '**glue ear**' or Otitis Media with Effusion (OME).

Bacterial and viral infections of the middle ear are also fairly common in children and are often associated with infections elsewhere, most commonly spreading from the throat. If the middle ear becomes infected, pus may collect in the middle ear cavity. This can cause extreme pain and pressure on the ear drum, causing it to tear and burst. This is one of the most common reasons for parents attending casualty departments with an inconsolable and feverish child. Once the drum has burst, however, the pressure is relieved and the child quietens. While the drum can naturally repair itself very quickly, repeated tearing can result in a build-up of scar tissue and small but permanent changes in hearing levels can remain. Middle ear infections can also occur as a complication of a malfunctioning Eustachian tube due to glue ear, or of inflammation of the membranes or enlarged tonsils and adenoids.

Treatment of middle ear problems

Treatment of early stage 'glue ear': Acute Otitis Media (AOM)

Two thirds of children will have at least one episode of AOM by their third birthday, and for most this will clear up by itself. For children over two years old who present at the GP surgery the management is usually to observe, and to treat any discomfort the child may experience with decongestants, offering mild pain relief if necessary. If the problem does not resolve within two days then antibiotics may be considered as a precaution against possible secondary infection. For AOM in a child under two years of age, antibiotic prescribing is the first line of treatment. Where AOM is recurrent or where it is associated with frequent or chronic upper respiratory chest infections or OME, then surgery may be considered (www.patient.co.uk/doctor/acute-otitis-media-in-children).

Treatment of later stages of 'glue ear': Otitis Media with Effusion (OME)

There have been many attempts to demonstrate which approaches are helpful in both improving children's hearing and also reducing any side effects such as language delay and behaviour difficulties. Treatment of OME can be divided into three approaches.

- Medical approaches

These include prescription of antibiotics, decongestants and steroids. There is no strong evidence base for any of these approaches.

- Non-surgical approaches

Children with Down's syndrome are more likely to have persistent OME, and where there is evidence of a hearing loss the approach is to manage this with hearing aids. Children with conditions associated with abnormal structures of the face and skull and who cannot wear ordinary hearing aids can be given specially designed hearing aids.

- Surgical approaches

The effectiveness of surgery for children with OME has been the subject of several large-scale reviews in recent years. The National Institute for Health and Clinical Excellence (NICE) supports the use of surgical intervention for children where there is documented evidence of OME persisting for three months or more and where hearing testing demonstrates a loss across a range of frequencies (www.nice.org.uk/nicemedia/live/11928/39564/39564.pdf).

The most common surgical intervention is the removal of secretions from the middle ear and the insertion of 'grommets' in one or both ears. A grommet is a tiny, hooked plastic tube that sits across the ear drum and acts as a permanently open window. Its function is to allow a free flow of air into the middle ear, particularly when the Eustachian tube is non-functioning. Where a child has an additional history of upper respiratory tract infections, the removal of adenoids is also recommended. Children get the most benefit from grommets in the first six to twelve months. Studies have shown that children with grommets will have better hearing and will spend more time 'effusion-free', but there is no convincing evidence that children who have had grommets inserted do any better when comparing language and cognitive development or behaviour.

What to look for in a child with hearing problems

The following points may alert a parent, an early years worker or a teacher to the possibility of a child having a hearing loss.

1 The child does not turn when called.
2 Hearing seems to fluctuate from day to day – sometimes the child will respond to speech at normal conversational levels, but at other times only to a 'shout'. Adults may report that the child 'hears when s/he wants to'.
3 The child seems particularly interested and attentive to visual cues – for example, watching the speaker's face.
4 The child's behaviour changes noticeably – for example, a normally friendly, settled child can become aggressive, tearful or withdrawn.
5 The child is distracted easily without one-to-one attention. In a group s/he may wander off or be a step behind the other children, watching to see what to do next.
6 The child responds very differently in quiet conditions compared to where there is a lot of background noise.
7 Language and speech development may be slowed down or seem to deteriorate after a cold. Speech may be hard to understand and the sentence structures the child uses may be simpler than those used by other children of a similar age.
8 The child may complain of painful or 'funny' ears, or pull at their ears.
9 The child may turn the TV volume up or choose to sit very near to the screen.
10 The child may speak louder or softer than usual.

Many of these features can also be noticed in children with speech, language and communication needs that are not directly related to hearing loss. If there is any concern about a child, it is essential that their hearing status is checked. Hearing loss needs to be ruled out so that the child's difficulties can be diagnosed.

Hearing loss and speech, language and communication development

The effect of PCHI from around birth has major implications for spoken language learning. Children with PCHI have a normal ability to acquire language, but because of their hearing impairment they may have difficulties both in understanding what is said and in being understood. Initially their language may seem to be similar to that expected of a younger child (see Chapter 2), but as the child grows the impact of a hearing loss may become evident in the development of understanding and use of speech and language. It is important to note that young children with PCHI can also often have additional temporary worsening of their hearing due to bouts of Otitis Media.

The impact on language development and communication of temporary conductive hearing loss due to middle ear problems is less clear. A great deal of research has been undertaken in an attempt to clarify the relationship. The outcomes can be summarised thus:

- approximately half of the children who are referred to speech and language therapists with delayed language development have a significant history of persistent Otitis Media;
- children with Otitis Media are more likely to have speech, language and communication difficulties when there is a second predisposing factor, such as birth difficulties or a family history of such difficulties. The difficulty that usually arises for children with Otitis Media is delayed development of speech, language and communication. For the majority of children this delay does not usually persist beyond Key Stage 1. The educational impact of the delay is sometimes seen in children who have difficulties developing literacy skills following a history of persistent Otitis Media in the early years.

In summary, the impact of Otitis Media would appear to depend on many factors including the frequency, severity and persistence of the hearing loss, other factors in the child's history that predispose them to speech, language and communication problems, and the personality of the child.

Identifying hearing problems

All babies born in the UK are offered a screening test of hearing within twenty eight days of birth in the Newborn Hearing Screening Programme (NHSP) (http://hearing.screening.nhs.uk). For babies born in hospital this will be offered before the mother and baby are discharged. For those born elsewhere or for those who missed their test in hospital the test can be carried out at home, in a community clinic or at a hearing test centre such as the paediatric audiology department of a hospital. For this screening test a quiet clicking sound is played into the infant's ear and the nerve response is measured on a small hand-held device. The test is designed to identify children with significant hearing loss. It will not pick up a mild-to-moderate hearing loss. It is very important that parents who do not have English as their first language are properly informed about the screening procedure.

Older children who seem to be having difficulty with hearing, listening or communication because of their behaviour in an everyday setting must also have their hearing tested. The Healthy Child Programme describes the role of health visitors in undertaking assessments of children's health and development during the pre-school years (www.gov.uk/government/uploads/system/uploads/attachment_data/file/219634/DFE-RR247-BCRP8.pdf).

The programme requires pre-school children to be assessed regularly to enable early identification of problems with development. Health visitors will use tools such as the Ages and Stages Questionnaire (ASQ 2014 http://agesandstages.com/) to identify any areas of concern, including attention and communication development.

However, passing an early hearing screening test does not guarantee that a child will have normal hearing. Occasionally children can slip through the net – for example, if their hearing loss is progressive, i.e. it gets worse as they get older. Some children may, for various reasons, miss out on the screening test. While children born in the UK are screened under the NHSP (and similar systems operate in many other countries), many children who have moved to the UK during their early years may not have had an early assessment of their hearing, and their hearing problems may only be picked up when they start attending nursery or school.

Formal assessment of hearing

If a child fails the screening test, s/he must be referred for a full diagnostic hearing assessment. If parents, early years workers or teachers are concerned about a child's hearing, at any stage, they can request that hearing is tested. This can be done via the child's GP or directly through the nearest hospital audiology department. A number of hearing tests are used, depending on the child's age. For children for whom English is an additional language (EAL) these tests do not require a knowledge of English. However, it is necessary for the audiologists to explain the testing procedures carefully for families with EAL. Some of the hearing tests are done using play techniques where the child is asked to respond to sounds.

These tests can take time. Other procedures are very quick, only requiring the child to sit still while their hearing is measured using clinical instruments, such as the test which indicates how well the middle ear is functioning. All the hearing test results should be included in the child's health records. As was the case for passing the screening test, the fact that a child has passed a diagnostic hearing test is not conclusive proof that they will have no hearing difficulties as they grow up. For example, a child with glue ear is likely to go through a cycle of disruption and recovery over a twelve-week period; the resulting hearing loss will fluctuate, so it may not be picked up on the day of the hearing test.

However, the fact that there is a temporary conductive hearing loss associated with glue ear can have a dramatic effect on the child's listening, attention and behaviour. Similarly, a PCHI affecting only one ear may have major implications for listening in the classroom, but this may not come to light until a child has failed to make progress in Literacy in Key Stages 1 or 2.

Early years provision and hearing problems

Staff in early years settings are likely to encounter a number of children at risk of hearing loss. This is partly because of the high incidence of Otitis Media in young children. Also, the close proximity of the children makes the spread of infections through the group more likely. In these settings there are several issues that may contribute to the difficulties experienced by children with hearing loss, and to the difficulties for staff in identifying a child with a possible hearing problem. Here are a few examples.

In some settings where many children are in the early stages of learning English as an additional language, staff may find it challenging to distinguish between possible hearing difficulties and difficulties understanding English. Access to a native speaker of the child's home language could be helpful in advising about the child's language development in their native language.

Noise levels where young children gather can be very high, and the noisy environment can make it extremely difficult for a child with a hearing problem to pick out speech signals. Such children may appear to misbehave, but in fact they cannot distinguish spoken instructions when there is too much noise. This could be especially difficult for children who are also struggling to understand English.

Given that there are generally poor staff–child ratios in most settings, it may be difficult for staff to be aware of an individual child's difficulties with hearing. For children with glue ear, some of their behaviour, such as aggression or tearfulness, may be attributable to their having trouble coping with changing hearing levels in a demanding, busy, social environment. (See Chapter 7 for more information about factors which affect a child's behaviour.)

Because language learning is taking place at such a rapid pace in this period, it is important to be aware when a child is having difficulty hearing the language spoken around them. If there is an awareness of the child's problems it is possible to provide an environment where staff can compensate for them in the ways in which interaction, learning and play are managed.

What to do if a hearing loss is suspected

1   If a child's behaviour suggests that they may not be hearing well, ask the parents whether the child had any hearing tests and what the results showed.
2   If hearing test results indicate any cause for concern, encourage the parents to seek further testing via their GP. Early years staff and/or parents can also refer the child directly to a local paediatric audiology department (NHS Choices www.nhs.uk/Conditions/Hearing-tests/).
3   Mention your concerns to the local child-health staff when they visit the early years provision.
4   Follow this up with enquiries regarding the results of any hearing assessments and request reports of the results.

Ways of helping a child with a hearing loss

There are many positive ways in which parents, early years workers and teachers can help a child with hearing loss, whether permanent or temporary.

1   Spend some time listening to the noise in the play rooms and class rooms. Is it all necessary? Can any be removed? Can quieter areas with soft coverings be set up? Can the window be closed for story time?
2   Try to ensure that a child with known or suspected hearing loss is placed towards the front of a group for group sessions – but not so near that it is hard to see the face of the speaker. Use horseshoe seating patterns rather than irregular rows so that children can see who is talking rather than having their back to the speaker.
3   Try to arrange the day's activities so that each child has some experience of listening in a small group, rather than having free play or large group activities only.
4   Maintain good lighting in the room and avoid sitting with your back to a window – your face will be in shadow.
5   It is essential to gain eye contact before beginning to talk to the child. Call their name first and pause until they look up, or use a phrase such as 'Are you ready, [name]?'
6   Make times for playing alongside a child, following their lead and interests. If possible, try to ensure that the child can see you and the objects they are playing with at the same time by being in their line of sight. This means getting to the child's level and getting joint attention on an object that you are talking about.

7 Try to include activities that require listening to speech and non-speech sounds – for example, marching to a drum, clapping when you hear your 'word' or name.

8 Try some listening games at quieter levels so that the child learns to use their hearing.

9 Ask a visiting speech and language therapist for some activity ideas for listening tasks and group games.

10 Offering a comment about what the child is doing is more effective at encouraging children to talk than asking a question (see Chapter 5).

11 When you've had your 'turn' in a conversation, make sure you give the child enough time to respond; children with hearing difficulties may need more time to process what you have said, so wait at least five seconds before you say anything further.

12 Share information about a child's hearing levels so that all adults can help to support the child and can also understand the child's behaviour.

Further reading/resources

www.ndcs.org.uk
This is the parent-friendly website of the National Deaf Children's Society. It gives basic information on hearing impairment, hearing aids and signing. There is a section on toys and books for children with PCHI, with names of suppliers.
http://hearing.screening.nhs.uk
This is the website of the UK Newborn Hearing Screening Programme.
www.nice.org.uk
This is the website for the National Institute for Clinical Excellence, which publishes all agreed national guidelines on best practice in medicine and healthcare.

Chapter 4

How to recognise speech, language and communication problems

Jannet A. Wright and Myra Kersner

Introduction

The normal pattern of speech and language development was outlined and the many varied aspects of human communication were described in Chapter 2. When the complexity of how speech and language develops is considered, it is amazing that the majority of children manage to enter the education system with communication skills that enable them to cope with the demands of school life. Even if some of these children were slow to acquire language initially, they will usually have 'caught up' during the pre-school years. However, there are some children whose poor speech, language and communication skills are a cause of anxiety to their parents and to the professionals who care for them, both before and after school entry.

This chapter is concerned with the early recognition of such children whose speech, language and communication is slow to develop and who are at risk of developing speech, language and communication needs (SLCN). Sometimes specific problem behaviours may be an indication that a child is having difficulties learning language, as discussed in Chapter 7. However, there may be some behaviour patterns which are not necessarily problematic in themselves but which may indicate that children are struggling with their speech and language development. It is these behaviours which will be described here. This might help parents and/or professionals caring for and working with such children to be aware of possible speech, language and communication problems, and to ask for specialist help for the child as early as possible in order to reduce the risk of them developing SLCN.

There are two important questions to be considered concerning the development of speech and language in children.

1 How well do they understand the language heard around them?
2 How well can they use speech and language so that other people know what they are saying?

In books about speech and language development, 'understanding' is frequently referred to as the **reception** or **comprehension** of language, and the output when a child attempts to speak as the **expression** of language. Comprehension and expression will be considered in turn, with guidelines and a checklist to highlight possible problems which may arise when learning language.

Comprehension

Some children have difficulty understanding what is said to them. This may be because they have problems with hearing (see Chapter 3), or because they are learning English as an additional language (EAL) and a different language is used at home – for example, where the parents are native speakers of Bengali, Cantonese, Turkish or Polish. However, even without hearing difficulties or problems associated with EAL, some children are slow in learning to talk, and their understanding of language is not as good as might be expected for their age.

Children who have problems in understanding are often helped by the 'clues' given to them by adult speakers. These clues may include pointing, gesture and facial expression.

Think about how much you can guess about what's going on when you visit a country where you don't know a word of the language. Children with poor understanding are in just that situation; they rely on these additional clues to help them make sense of what is going on around them. They watch the faces of adults, and from watching the facial expressions they will know if an adult is cross with them or if the adult is pleased about something they have done. However, there are children who have problems in social interaction who find it difficult or impossible to understand anything from the facial expressions of the adults and children around them (see Chapter 8).

To help you think about this further, try giving someone directions about a route they have to follow without using your hands. It is harder than you think; we do not always realise how much we use our hands to support what we are saying.

Children use the gestures and facial expressions that accompany speech to help them work out a situation, so it is difficult for us to know exactly how much speech and language a child understands. Two teachers were heard to make the following observations about Ben:

'He understands everything that's going on.'
'He doesn't understand a word I say.'

These comments seem to be in total disagreement, but in fact both may be true. Ben probably could understand everything that was going on by watching for the clues or because the situation was very familiar to him, but he may not have understood much of what the second teacher actually said. Thus, if he is told to go and line up by the door when he knows it is time for lunch, he will follow the other children and carry out the familiar routine without needing to understand the actual spoken words. However, an unexpected question such as 'Have you got a pet at home, Ben?' might well be met with nothing more than a blank stare.

Children with poor understanding often work extremely hard to try and follow instructions and keep up with what is happening in a group. One way they may help themselves to cope and manage the situation will be to watch other children and copy them. In the classroom this may mean that they are the last to start an activity or follow an instruction because they are waiting to see what the other children do before they start work or respond to an instruction. They may attend to, or hear, only the last word or words in a sentence and appear to ignore part of what was said. So, they may look as though they are being disobedient or not concentrating.

The situation within the home or early years setting may provide additional clues about the problems such a child might be experiencing. For example, the instruction 'Put your coat on, Joshua' may be accompanied by the speaker pointing to the coat-rack or holding out the coat, or the instruction may be given at a time when all the other children are putting on coats because it is home-time. Similarly, questions may be asked or instructions given relating to various activities, when the objects being talked about are in front of or near to the child. For example:

- 'Find the red engine, Matthew,' when there are a variety of different coloured engines.
- 'Jacinta, where are the scissors?' when involved in a task where she needs to cut something.
- 'What are you doing to teddy, Tyler?' when he is holding a teddy.

The same may happen with general instructions, such as those given below, which are all part of the routine of the day, and which most children quickly learn without needing to understand the individual words. They just follow what others are doing or what they know the situation requires without really listening to what is said.

For example:

- 'It's tidy-up time.'
- 'Wash your hands for dinner.'
- 'Come and sit down for story time.'

Children will respond to these instructions without needing to understand all the words because they indicate a familiar routine or pattern of behaviour.

When talking to children, adults are for the most part unaware of how much help is provided by such contextual or situational clues; they occur naturally and without our thinking about them too much.

In order to establish how much spoken language a child is actually understanding, it is necessary to try and eliminate all these additional, helpful clues, and to assess the child's ability to comprehend using words alone.

When children are learning to talk it is quite common for them to repeat what they have just heard. This is part of learning and is to be encouraged. However, as a child gets older, if they continue to 'echo' what was said to them and constantly repeat what adults or children are saying, this may indicate that they have a serious comprehension problem, as illustrated below:

> Nursery teacher: 'Is it your birthday today?'
> Child: 'Birthday.'
> Nursery teacher: 'Yes, you're four today!'
> Child: 'Four today.'
> Nursery teacher: 'Did you have many presents?'
> Child: 'Many presents.'

The child here is apparently not understanding because she is merely echoing the words, not answering the questions.

What to look for

- The child who is slow to learn the class routine.
- The child who watches and copies others.
- The child with poor attention at story time.
- The child who 'echoes'.
- The child who often makes an inappropriate response to questions and instructions.
- The child who does not seem too interested in or does not respond to people's facial expressions.

Although these may be indicators of a problem, they cannot be used as the only means of identification as these behaviours could also indicate that the child has learning difficulties and/or a lack of confidence. The problem needs to be investigated in more detail.

How to check

- Give simple instructions such as 'Go and get a book' without clues, and note the child's response.

- Ask the occasional question 'out of the blue', which does not relate to anything the child has just been doing.
- Give more complex directions and possibly unexpected instructions, and note exactly what the child does. For example: 'Go to the cupboard and get a piece of blue paper'; or 'put a piece of LEGO on the table before you go outside.'

What to do

- Ask for the child's hearing to be checked (see Chapter 3).
- All professionals need to be aware of the language(s) spoken at home.
- Refer to a speech and language therapist.
- Use the child's name when giving an instruction. This will gain their attention as they may not realise initially that the instruction applies to them as well.
- Watch closely to see if the child's response is appropriate for your instructions. Do this on several occasions in different contexts and write down exactly what the child does, as this will help you see if there is a pattern to the way in which they respond to instructions.
- Use short simple instructions.
- Make use of everyday gesture to aid understanding.

Expression

There are a number of important aspects of speech and language, all of which are necessary in order to be understood when talking to other people. These are:

- the sounds (**articulation**), which make up
- the words (**vocabulary**) which must be in
- the right order (**syntax** or **grammar**) and
- appropriate to the situation (**pragmatics**).

If any of these areas are slow to develop, then communication may break down. The child will not be able to get their message across, and this can become a serious problem as the child gets older.

Each of these areas will be considered in turn.

Articulation

This area is concerned with a child's mastery of the sounds of the language. Young children take time, literally, to get their tongues round the sounds of the language, and many – but not all – children practise these sounds in the babbling stage of infancy, as described in Chapter 2. Some sounds are easier to make than others:

/m/ as in mummy, more
/n/ as in nana, no
/b/ as in baby, bye
/d/ as in daddy

These are all quite straightforward and are usually the first sounds a child produces.

Slightly more difficult sounds are:

/k/ (written also as 'c') as in kitten, car
/g/ as in go

while the following sounds are all quite difficult and usually develop after the sounds referred to above:

/f/ as in finger
/v/ as in van
/s/ as in sun, sea
/ch/ as in chip
/r/ as in rabbit
/sh/ as in shoe, ship, sugar

Words and phrases in which a number of these more difficult sounds occur together require the tongue and lips to perform some quite difficult gymnastics. In a word like 'nana' there are only two sounds, which are repeated, and the tongue does not have a great deal to do, but in a phrase such as 'fish and chips' there are nine different sounds:

'f- i- sh - a-n- ch-i-p-s' = nine sounds

(Note that when talking quickly you rarely say/hear the 'd' at the end of 'and'.) All of this involves the tongue in some tricky manoeuvres. Try saying 'fish and chips' slowly to yourself and think about how you do it.

It is therefore not at all uncommon or surprising to hear young children producing common immaturities such as:

'wabbit' for rabbit
'tip' for chip
'pi' or 'pit' for fish

Sometimes they get some of the sounds right but put them in the wrong place. For example, Adrianna aged three years could say:

'tis an fips' (fish and chips)

She managed the difficult /s/ and /f/ sounds, but got them in the wrong order. Other examples of getting sounds the wrong way round in a word are:

'efalant' elephant
'tefalone' telephone
'hostipul' hospital

Other common immaturities include:

'tar' car
'dot' got

and words in which the tongue comes forward in a lisp, as in:

'thun' sun
'thock' sock

Sometimes children miss the /s/ at the beginning of some words, for example:

'poon' spoon
'tar' star
'carf' scarf

This is because the second sound of the word is a **consonant** and the tongue and lips have some difficult manoeuvres to make. It is easier to say words in which a **vowel** follows a consonant, as in:

'c a r'   's a y'   't oo l'   'n ai l'

than to say words where two consonants occur next to each other, as in:

'sc a r'   'st a y'   'st oo l'   'sn ai l'

especially when one of the two consonants in the consonant cluster is the difficult /s/ sound.

By the time children approach their fourth birthday many of the immature pronunciations should have disappeared, or there may still be some residual influences if another language is spoken at home.

Phonology

This is related to articulation and the speech sounds of language. The word 'phonology' is used by speech and language therapists to refer to the way in which individual sounds are put together to make words within a given language, such that changing a sound within a word will change the meaning. For example, children learn quite early on that there is a difference between:

'*p*ear' and '*b*ear'
'*c*at' and '*h*at'
'mou*th*' and 'mou*se*'
'p*u*ppy' and 'p*o*ppy'
'Da*nn*y' and 'Da*dd*y'
'dog' and 'dog*s*'

By changing (or adding) one sound in each of these pairs of words (known as **minimal pairs**) there is a resultant change of meaning.

Most children learn how the sound system of the language works, but how they do this is one of the wonders of child language development. Nobody teaches them how to recognise that different sounds make different meanings; they learn the rules of phonology in much the same way as they work out for themselves the rules of grammar.

The examples of the immature pronunciations given earlier showed that, although young children may be aware of how sounds in a language work together to make words and change meaning and how different combinations of sounds affect the meaning, in the early years some children may not have the necessary ability to put their lips and tongues around the sounds to give the complete adult pronunciation.

Other children may have different problems. Children with hearing problems (see Chapter 3) will have difficulty hearing the small differences that carry meaning; they may therefore be unable to produce some of the sounds accurately, thus making their speech hard to understand. Some children whose hearing for everyday sounds seems adequate may have particular difficulty in distinguishing the small differences between specific sounds such as /p/ and /b/, or /f/ and /v/. Also sounds like 'tr' as in '*tr*ain' and 'ch' as in '*ch*ain' may sound alike unless you listen closely. Speech and language therapists therefore use tests containing sets of minimal pairs of words to check how well children hear and discriminate the differences between them.

Some children, although they are able to discriminate speech sounds, nonetheless use only a few sounds to do the work of many. Gary aged three years nine months used the /g/ sound most of the time. For example, he would say:

'I wan go geep bu egun maging goig.'
[I want(to) go (to) sleep but everyone (is) making (a) noise.]

He uses the [g] sound instead of /sl/ in 'sleep', /v/ in 'everyone', /k/ in 'making' and /z/ at the end of 'noise'. He also missed some words out – see **syntax** below.

All this makes his speech very hard to understand. His mother can understand him, but other family members and friends often have to ask for a translation. This is because his mother has got used to Gary's style of pronunciation. People who are in daily contact with such children may become familiar with their unusual speech. This does not necessarily mean that the children are speaking more clearly, but that the listener has become more used to their speech patterns.

These speech patterns are called *phonological systems*; a child such as Gary may have his own phonological system which changes and develops as he gradually acquires more sounds, and as he learns to fit these sounds together to match the adult phonological system of the language. Not all children manage this task; they are then described as having a *phonological disorder*.

Phonological disorders may occur in different ways. For example, there are children who may not have all of the sounds, like Deepal aged four who said:

'Dit my pable, I'm puttin tup om it.'
[This (is) my table, I'm putting cup(s) on it.]

However, other children may have most or all of the sounds, but use them so variably that they remain unintelligible. If in addition they omit certain sounds, the result is a problem for the listener. This sentence from Michelle, aged seven, is an example:

'You dot one bat tipey tot an one bap potty pok.'

meaning:

'You've got one black stripey sock and one black spotty sock.'

It is important to remember that while many children grow out of early speech difficulties, some need help before they get to school, where teachers and other children expect them to be able to communicate clearly. Simple problems like lisping, which usually affects the s and sh sounds, may sort themselves out, but parents, teachers and early years workers need to be alert to children such as Gary and Deepal, who have more complex speech, language and communication needs (SLCN). Some children who have speech difficulties which are complex, severe or unusual may later experience difficulty with reading, writing and spelling. For further reading on this topic, see Simpson (2012).

What to look for

- The child who is difficult to understand.
- The child who cannot be understood by adults outside the family.
- The child whose speech sounds 'muddled'.
- The child who appears to have only a few sounds.
- The child who says the same word differently at different times.
- The child who does not make distinctions between the words as you would expect.

How to check

- Look at a book or pictures with a child in a quiet corner and listen to him/her. It is important to listen carefully because it is easy to think the child has said a word correctly when you have understood what s/he has said.
- Name pictures for the child and encourage him/her to imitate you – notice how each word is said.

What to do

- Ask for the child's hearing to be checked.
- Check whether other family and friends understand the child's speech.
- Refer to a speech and language therapist.
- Do not mimic the child to their face.
- Say the word correctly in a sentence following their incorrect attempt, but do not repeat the incorrect pronunciation to the child.

Vocabulary

Some children do not have the words or vocabulary which one might expect for their age. For example, Lucas aged six years was looking at a book with his mother.

> Mother: 'Oh look, there's a...'
> Lucas: 'That.'
> Mother: 'Yes, it's a car.'
> Lucas: 'Car.'
> Mother: 'They're going on the...'
> Lucas: 'That.'
> Mother: 'Yes, the road.'

When talking about the pictures Lucas appears not to have the vocabulary to describe what he sees in the picture. He is six years old and he should have been able to do this type of activity. Usually by the age of four years a child is able to use nouns to name objects that they can see in a picture, and use verbs to talk about some of the actions.

Children's first words are awaited with eager anticipation by the adults around them; they are often recorded in a book. When children are first learning to talk their parents can easily remember the words they can say. However, very quickly it becomes impossible to keep track as their vocabulary grows at such a rapid rate.

An activity such as the one Lucas is doing, naming pictures in a book, is often more appropriate with children in the first two to three years of life. It provides them with the opportunity to learn and practise new words. This is why they frequently choose the same book for adults to read to them, so that they have a chance to practise or rehearse new vocabulary. By the time they are six years old (Lucas's age) they are usually more interested in listening to and retelling a story.

Children who appear to have difficulty learning new words, or remembering words, could have a language delay. Their speech may sound clear and their sentence structures appear appropriate for what they want to say, but their vocabulary may not be increasing in the way one would expect.

What to look for

- A child who finds it hard to remember the names of objects and the names of other children in the class.
- A child who has trouble learning new words.
- A child who uses 'this'/'that' a great deal when referring to items/objects and does not say the name of the object or item.
- A child who is not always fluent (see Chapter 6).

How to check

- Choose an unfamiliar book or toy to look at with the child. After talking about a few of the pictures or items, see if the child can tell you what they are. Try again the next day, and again the day after.
- If a child cannot name an object, see if he/she can tell you what it is used for.

What to do

- Choose a topic such as fruit, clothes, transport or animals and draw the child's attention to certain words during a week. See if they remember the specific words in a week and then in two weeks' time.

- Find out if remembering or learning new words is a problem in other situations – for example, early years settings, school or with grandparents.
- Ask the speech and language therapist to see the child.
- See Chapters 9 and 10.

Syntax

Sam, aged four years, explained how his father was carrying out some do-it-yourself.

'My dad out went hammer, got hammer wood got down.'

Sam manages to get his message across, but the words are not in the order we would expect. It sounds strange. In English words are put in a certain order in a sentence; this is the grammar or syntax of the language. If children have difficulties in this area their sentences may be very short in length or they may sound 'odd' because the order is incorrect. Sometimes children talk using the correct sounds, and as the adult can understand what they are saying, it is easy to ignore the fact that the words are not in the right order. The following sentence shows this:

Elaina, aged five years: 'Mummy, ice-cream me have?'
Mother: 'Later, when we go to the shops.'

Elaina's mother understands that Elaina is asking for an ice-cream because she is used to Elaina's syntax, but to a stranger this would sound unusual.

It is more common for children to have both poor articulation and poor syntax, which makes it very difficult for the listener to understand their speech, as in the examples of Gary and Deepal given earlier in this chapter.

Telegrammatic speech

Sometimes when listening to a very young child or an older child who has difficulty with syntax the listener is aware that the child's speech sounds rather like a verbal telegram. When telegrams were used to send messages the cost increased with the number of words, so there was an art in getting the message across in as few as words as possible to save money. For example, 'Arrived safe (stop) back Tuesday (stop)'. A child who has difficulty with syntax/grammar may produce sentences that sound like a telegram, and in fact this type of speech has been called telegrammatic speech. You can see why if you read the examples below:

'Me go school now' instead of 'I go to school now'
'Daddy go work car' instead of 'Daddy goes to work in the car'

In these examples the children retain the words which carry the information in the sentence rather like a telegram, but miss out the small linking words like 'the' and 'and'. However, if children have a problem with syntax, they are unlikely to leave out words from choice; it is more likely that they cannot cope with a longer utterance, or that they have failed to learn the linking words. They may not understand the importance of such words and they may not be able to hear them.

The linking words in the phrases above include 'to', 'in' and 'the'. If a child is two years old the omission of these linking words would not cause concern. At this age children string together the important words so that when telling an adult what they intend to do, 'Me go garden' is perfectly acceptable. However, if a child is still doing this at four years old there would be cause for concern, because at this age you would expect to hear 'I want to go in the garden'.

The following example indicates a severe problem in a five-year-old boy, describing an outing with his parents:

'Mummy, daddy, me went car, long time, shops, ice-cream, new shirt.'

This child gets his message across, but the listener has to do a lot of work in order to understand that he meant:

- Mummy, daddy and child went in the car;
- it was a long way to town;
- the child had an ice-cream in a restaurant;
- a new shirt was bought for the child.

If you suspect a child is having problems with syntax, the following suggestions may help.

What to look for

- A child missing words out of a sentence.
- A child who gets words in the wrong order in a sentence.
- A child whose speech sounds a bit like a telegram.

How to check

- Listen carefully to children when they are telling a story, or talking about something they have just done.
- Note down exactly what they say, do not add in any extra words.
- Look at your notes; have they left any words out? Or are any of the words in an order that surprises you?

What to do

- Provide the correct, full-length version of the child's sentence after they have spoken to you, but do not expect them to repeat it. (See 'Modelling', Chapter 2.)
- Ask a speech and language therapist to see the child.
- Do not mimic the child's speech.

Children who have problems, or who are delayed in learning to talk, often have all these types of difficulty at the same time: difficulties with sounds, with vocabulary and with syntax. These are the children who are 'reluctant communicators', who say little, often only speaking one or two words at a time, who point and use gesture to help them 'ask' for what they want, and who are unwilling to talk with people they do not know well.

Pragmatics – the use of language

Pragmatics refers to the use of language and how we choose an appropriate way of talking, depending on the situation we find ourselves in. You might ask a child to shut the door by saying:

'Shut the door please, Ashraf.'

To an adult you might say any of these:

'Could you shut the door?'
'Would you mind shutting the door?'
'Do you want to shut the door?'

You probably use a different style of speech with adults you know well, such as family members and friends when you might just say ' shut the door', than with those you are meeting for the first time when you will automatically use more polite language. Children usually learn these differences quite unconsciously, but some children have to be taught the appropriate use of language so they know which style of speech to use in a particular setting.

Conversation is not just two people talking, each saying something in turn; what they say should be linked in some way. If it is not linked, it is like a crossed line on the telephone with two unconnected conversations going on.

A normal conversation with a four year old would go something like this:

Sabita, aged four years: 'I got new shoes.'
Nursery teacher: 'Did you? How nice.'
Sabita: 'Yes, they're red.'
Nursery teacher: 'Where did you get them?'
Sabita: 'My mum and me went to the shop.'

Now look at this conversation between Tracy aged five years and her teacher:

Tracy: 'I got new shoes.'
Teacher: 'Did you? How nice.'
Tracy: 'I got new shoes.'
Teacher: 'I know, you just told me.'
Tracy: 'I'm doing painting now.'

This conversation is not as successful as the one with Sabita, and it is typical of Tracy's conversations with adults and children. Tracy knows how to attract adult attention, but she cannot maintain the conversation. A successful continuation of this exchange would probably have involved Tracy pointing to the shoes and getting the adult to look at them, instead of repeating her first statement.

When talking to children who have difficulty in the area of pragmatics, a number of features may be apparent. They may have particular difficulty in linking their responses to the other speaker's comments. For example, when doing some craft work at school, the teacher said, 'Look, the paper has stuck to the table.' The response from the child was, 'We've got yellow tables like this at home' – words that make sense but are not appropriate for that particular conversational exchange.

Children with such difficulties are poor at taking turns in a conversation, so they constantly interrupt and their comments are not related. It is normal for young children to interrupt if they see or hear something novel, such as a fire engine going by, but by school entry, constant interruptions and inappropriate comments may signal a problem. Such children may also have difficulty taking turns in games in the classroom or any group activities.

They may not know how to attract the adult's attention when starting a conversation. Children without any problems may call out to the adult passing by, or say, 'Guess what!' 'Look!' or 'See this,' or they may pull an adult's sleeve. A child who finds it difficult or who is unable to attract adult attention may start talking without looking at the adult. It may sound as if they are talking to themselves. The adult eventually becomes aware that the child is talking to them and that a response is needed.

They may not know how to talk about a person or object which is not present. Such children assume that the listener knows what they are referring to. To the listener it may feel like they are coming into a conversation half way through. They may also not understand exactly what the listener could be expected to know and not know about the topic under discussion or the situation they are referring to – for example, a child may come in from playing outside and make reference to something that happened that the teacher could not be expected to know about.

Such children may have difficulty linking topics in a conversation, and if the conversation breaks down they do not know how to start it up again or 'repair' it. They will also have difficulties knowing how to end a conversation – how to conclude if that is required, or even what words to use in order to leave the situation.

What to look for

- A child who has problems taking turns in a conversation.
- A child whose conversation continually moves from one topic to the next, fairly rapidly, for no reason.
- A child who cannot switch topics and goes on and on about a subject.
- An educational setting which may be adding to the child's problems. The adult's language may be too complex, or there may not be enough time for the child to understand what is said to them and for them to respond.
- A child who is not interested in playing with other children.
- A child who appears to have difficulty in developing imaginative play.
- A child whose responses are inappropriate.

How to check

- Listen to the child in conversation with another adult.
- Listen to the child in conversation with another child, and with a group of children.
- Watch how the child gets adult attention.
- Note if the child is able to take turns in the conversation.
- Look at the complexity of the adult's language. This may be causing a breakdown in communication, because the child does not understand what the adult is saying.

What to do

- Initially, if a child does interrupt all the time, make it clear to the child that they must wait their turn and not interrupt other speakers. Then monitor how quickly they learn this rule and/or whether they can manage to learn it.
- Make clear the rules of behaviour at home or within the classroom.
- This is a very complex area of communication to help. It is therefore best to ask a speech and language therapist to see the child, although information you have gathered about the child's communication and behaviour will be helpful to the therapist.

- In some cases a speech and language therapist may ask parents to complete the Checklist for Autism in Toddlers (CHAT: Baron-Cohen et al. 2000) at the eighteen-month developmental check.

Summary

This chapter outlines some of the reasons why it can be hard to identify a child who has difficulty understanding speech and language.

Examples are given of problems which can occur with articulation, vocabulary, syntax and pragmatics.

It is important to remember that, as listeners, we are very good at interpreting what we hear people say to us. When talking with children, the most important aspect is listening to what they say, so we can respond appropriately. However, in order to watch out for potential difficulties, we also have to learn to listen to how they say it.

Adults who work with children are in the frontline of identifying speech and language problems. It is often the child's behaviour, such as temper tantrums and/or withdrawal from speech situations, that cause adults to suspect a delay in development.

References

Baron-Cohen, S., Wheelwright, S., Cox, A., Baird, G., Charman, T., Swettenham, J., Drew, A. and Doehring, P. (2000) Early Identification of Autism by the Checklist for Autism in Toddlers (CHAT) *Journal for the Royal Society of Medicine*, 93 (10), 521–525.
Simpson, S. (2012) (2nd edition) Working with Children with Written Language Difficulties. In M. Kersner and J.A. Wright (Eds.) *Speech and Language Therapy: the decision-making process when working with children*. London: Routledge.

Further reading

Lancaster, G. (2007) *Developing Speech and Language Skills: Phoneme Factory*. London: Routledge.
Speake, J. and Barnes, R. (2003) *How to Identify and Support Children with Speech and Language Difficulties*. Wisbech: LDA.

Chapter 5

Working with parents

Keena Cummins

Working with parents is informative, challenging and – even more importantly – fundamental. As practitioners such as early years workers, speech and language therapists and psychologists, our objective is to do all we can to 'help children have the best possible start in life' (EYFS 2012 www. foundationyears.org.uk/eyfs-statutory-framework/). We need to ensure that parents know how capable they are as their child's communicative partner, and how together we can support children in developing strong self-esteem, resilience and independence both communicatively and in everyday life. Some of the ideas in this chapter about how to work with parents draw on the experience of Cummins and Hulme (2001).

In all cultures, from the moment of birth children provide strong communication signals, with their head, face, eyes, hands and voice. Parents intuitively reinforce and extend these signals, thereby stretching the child to the next phase of their communicative development. This leads to a positive two-way sharing of control which in turn leads to further experimentation and reinforcement, that then helps to build confidence and self-belief. The child presents opportunities for communication and learning and the parent and child together build on (scaffold) one another's ideas.

The impact of communication difficulties

Children with communication difficulties are not as consistent, clear or effective in providing signals as their peers. This makes it harder for parents to know how to respond. It becomes difficult for parents to know what to reinforce, and this in turn affects the child's wish to experiment with their communication. If each misses the other's timing, the synchrony of their interaction starts to erode. This affects the confidence of both parent and child, masking their intuitive skills, and has an impact on their self-esteem. The parent may try to repair the interaction by taking the dominant role and over-compensating. Each time the adult predicts what the child is trying to say the child's need to communicate diminishes, which may then promote 'learned helplessness'.

Parents' responses

Parents of children with speech, language and communication needs (SLCN) are not a homogenous group in terms of culture, personality or coping strategies. Each will differ with regard to their response to their child's communication difficulties and their reaction to its severity. Some people appear to manage their child's particularly complex needs with ease, whereas others are overwhelmed even by a mild delay. Some parents will be aware of a child's diagnosis from birth, whereas for others their child's communication difficulties may not become apparent until much later.

Parents' responses are affected by their values and beliefs, their own personal experiences, their support network and the ever-changing complexities and pressures of their daily lives. The parents of a child with SLCN may do the same things as they did with their other children, in terms of communication, and yet that child may not appear to progress at the same rate. Parents may appear on the surface to be confident and assured or uninterested and disengaged, but when they are provided with empathic opportunity they will frequently report a range of emotions.

For example:

- Sadness – 'Poor them.'
- Concern – 'What does this mean for my child?'
- Anger – 'What has gone wrong?' 'Who is to blame?'
- Guilt – 'What have I done wrong?'
- Frustration – 'Why can't I understand what he is indicating or saying?'
- Irritation – 'Why can't he just do/say it?'
- Remorse – 'Why did I get cross?'
- Fear – 'If I mention this to anyone, will it become real? Will I lose control of my child's future?'
- Denial – 'If I ignore it, will it sort itself out?'
- Judged – 'They think I am a bad parent.'
- Unsure – 'I don't know what to do.'
- Hurt – 'My child doesn't seem to love me.'
- Defeatist – 'What's the point?'

Parents may feel that their family dynamics and social networks are changing due to others, including relatives and friends, reacting differently, which may lead to conflict. They may feel anxious about the balance of time spent with each of their children and with their partner. They may also worry about the implications these difficulties may have on their child's general social life and future opportunities. These emotions can become debilitating, leading to feelings of inadequacy and confusion. They may significantly affect how the parents feel about themselves, their child and their own relationships.

Vulnerability

A child with communication difficulties may have all or just one area of their communication development affected, but they will characteristically find it difficult to engage in an interaction or to be understood. It might appear as if they are not listening, not responding, are not interested or are choosing to be difficult. These patterns of behaviour frequently lead to misunderstandings and subjective and judgemental statements where the child is labelled as being 'shy', 'naughty' or 'bored'. These words do not reflect the child's state accurately and are not productive for the child's developing self-identity.

If parents notice other people struggling when engaging with their child they may try to anticipate or repair any potential misunderstandings. They may try to compensate by leading interactions in order to protect their child. Some parents frequently fill silences with questions and commentary and support their child by doing things for them. Others may try to avoid social situations. They may feel permanently 'wired' as they anticipate and try to resolve situations, and consequently will often feel exhausted.

Of course, parents of children with SLCN are no less skilled than any other parents. They are frequently offered support and advice that is sensitive, productive and supportive. At other times they may receive advice that appears to be irritating, patronising and ill-informed. When trying to follow such advice they may even appear to be negating their own child's behaviour. Parents find they are continuously explaining to others about their child, feeling the need to manage others' opinions and perceptions. They may try to respond without offending but often, when they are saying what they feel they need to say, they may come across as being defensive or confrontational.

Seeking support

We are all strongly influenced by what we have learnt from our parents and our own experiences within our society. How we seek support depends on our past experiences. We need to feel we are of equal value to others in order to deal with the situations in which we find ourselves and to trust those who are there to support us. Meeting new people can be daunting for a parent if their confidence is low. They may have negative experiences of social groups, education, health and social services, or they may have been unwell, either physically or with post-natal depression, for example. This may be a particular problem if they have learned English as an additional language. It may also be difficult if they have concerns about how they and their child will be perceived, or if they do not fully understand the local health, education and social service systems.

National agenda

The drive to deliver quality early years provision with free access has meant that increasing numbers of families are being provided with an accessible environment that offers welcoming, culturally respectful and language-rich opportunities for their child. This has been developed in an attempt to reduce the previously separated and segregated support services that led to parents attending appointments in a confusing variety of settings.

With regard to the development of speech, language and communication, the Royal College of Speech and Language Therapists supports the need for speech and language therapy services to be delivered collaboratively. It emphasises the importance of good working relationships between parents, different agencies, communities and schools in the context most functionally relevant to the child and their family (RCSLT 2006). It is essential for individual professionals to fulfil this.

The statutory Early Years Foundation Stage Framework for Learning (EYFS 2014) (www.gov.uk/government/publications/early-years-founda tion-stage-profile-handbook-2014) prioritises equality of opportunities for all children and parents. It stresses the need for collaboration of practitioners in all early years settings, and makes explicit the importance of developing communication and language skills. It provides a collaborative observation tool with guidance materials and developmental descriptions for use with each child in different settings. This enables practitioners to reflect on and monitor the child's developing skills. They can then feed back their observations to parents and provide information for other practitioners.

Individualised support

Whatever our role as practitioners when working with children with SLCN, in order to provide optimal support for children, we need to appear relaxed and unpressured, and be able to spend dedicated time with them. We need to be able to describe the specific behaviours and development of the children while demonstrating that we enjoy working with them.

We need to make every effort to support the parents' access to the environment. This could be through the use of an advocate, or where English is an additional language, with the help of an interpreter, a bilingual co-worker or a family friend translating. We need to build a reciprocal relationship with the parents, listening to their knowledge, insights and anecdotes in order to fully understand about the children, their families and what is beneficial for them. We need to learn about the parents' strengths and learn to respect the family's values. Developing empathy with the family is fundamental and is best achieved through the seminal Rogerian principles of offering 'unconditional positive regard' (Rogers 1951). This means providing our full attention and being open, honest and non-judgemental in any discussions we may hold. It also means sensitively sharing the knowledge and experience we have gained through our professional role and reflecting on our own interactions with the child.

'The Reflective Practitioner' (Schon 1983)

Practitioners are as strongly influenced as any adult by their upbringing and experiences and therefore are as prone as anyone to stereotyping, potential biases and making judgements. Successful facilitation of communication for the children they work with is based on understanding their own perceptions, beliefs and behaviours as well as those that are prevalent in the children's world.

In order to become truly 'reflective practitioners', as early years workers we need to ask ourselves several key questions.

Questions about beliefs

- What are our own values and life-goals?
- How do we prioritise the additional demands made on families in terms of time, lifestyle and finance?
- How do we feel about different family structures and makeup – for example, single parents, same-sex parents, extended families, reconstituted 'blended' families, teenage parents?
- What beliefs do we hold about different cultures and families from varying socio-economic backgrounds?
- How do we feel about others' beliefs and practices?
- How do we respond to a parent's feelings and their emotional state?
- Do we believe in parents' equality with practitioners and do we recognise parents' intuitive skills?

Questions about role

- What do we think our role is in supporting the children – for example, are you a supporter, facilitator or teacher?
- Who do we think has the knowledge – parents or practitioners?
- What do we think we can gain/learn from working with parents?
- How do we feel about children with speech, language and communication difficulties?
- How do we feel about children with challenging behaviour?
- How do we find out about parents' knowledge and skills?
- How do we feel about particular children we are working with?

Questions about language

- How do we make ourselves equally accessible to families where English is not their first language?
- How do we identify and select meaningful vocabulary matching that which would be used by the family?
- How do we describe the children we are working with – for example, do we concentrate on their strengths and their emerging skills or describe only the characteristics of their difficulties?
- Do we avoid using subjective words such as 'shy' or 'naughty' and use positive descriptors such as 'increasing in confidence' and 'developing their attention'?
- How do we describe the children's patterns of behaviour?
- When are descriptive 'labels' useful and when and how do we use them?
- How much verbal information do we provide and when do we provide it?
- How and when do we check whether the parents have understood the verbal information we have given them?

Questions about non-verbal signals

- How do we select the environment in which to speak to the parents – for example, at home or in the nursery?
- How do we set up the environment in which to speak to the parents? For example, are they seen in a confidential setting? How do we arrange the chairs? Do we provide adult-size chairs? Do we offer any refreshments?
- How much time do we allow in which to listen and understand?
- How much do we allow our anxiety to influence our interaction with the parents – for example, through our facial expression, the rate of our speech or the tone of our voice?
- Have we reflected on our own interaction skills?
- Do we monitor our own interaction skills with the child and with the parents?

Competition

There is a natural competitive element within any group setting. This may be between two children, between a child and an adult or between any number of children within a larger group.

Children often have to compete for adult attention and some children know how to attract this attention and become the focus of the adults. In such cases it is not difficult to give positive feedback to the parents. The frequent interactions with adults of a vociferous child make them easy to remember. If the parents of such children then receive specifically encouraging feedback they may leave the early years setting with positive feelings.

However, children with SLCN may have reduced opportunities to secure attention for themselves. They may be overshadowed, the opportunities for communication having been sabotaged by more forthright children who may even be their own siblings. They may find their attempts to attract attention difficult, often appearing 'not to engage', or they may make extra attempts such as by crying or through some negative behaviour.

Such behaviour may have an impact on how we as practitioners feel about the child and how and what we feed back to the parents. For example, if we feel anxious, frustrated or irritable we might give the parent very negative feedback. As a result, parents of children with SLCN may frequently leave the early years setting having received reports of concerns, negative observations, or general statements such as 'He was fine today', which inadvertently highlights the vulnerabilities of the child rather than focussing on the child's emerging strengths.

Practitioners frequently report that they wonder if they have given these children enough time. They feel unclear about the abilities of the child with SLCN, and feel unsure whether they are supporting them sufficiently. They may not know what to do to ensure all the children have equal opportunities. They would not wish to inhibit the more confident child, but they want to increase the opportunities for the child with SLCN to engage with them as this will help to build the child's confidence and enable them to access as many interaction opportunities as possible.

Within an early years setting, once a child has been seen to have problems there is a risk of everyone focussing on those difficulties. In some cases this may propagate the perception of a 'difficult' child. If this perception is maintained the adults may focus on the child's weaker areas and accentuate them. However, if the child can be described in terms of what they can do, with the focus shifting to accentuate their emerging skills, the perception of people within the setting may be changed. This offers more opportunity for the child. The vocabulary we use has a profound impact on how others perceive the child. For example, if we say the child is 'obsessive' people may make assumptions about the child being 'rigid' in some way, whereas if we describe them as being 'passionate' about certain things, people may perceive them as being highly focussed and interested.

Filtering

Communication in the current world is very rapid and is likely to be over stimulating for children with SLCN.

Recent advances in neuroscience suggest that from birth the neurons in our brains are being triggered rapidly by all stimuli and are laying down connections and feedback loops that are continuously firing, interlinking and making connections. Children who communicate with ease are able to pick out and focus on significant information consistently. They can screen out the less important information and by choosing what they pay attention to, can lay down consistent neural maps. However, children with SLCN appear to need support in picking out the salient information and structuring it appropriately.

In all cultures a child's development is supported through their attachment to their parents who help them to filter information and to notice the significant things in their environment.

As adults we perceive ourselves to be good at 'filtering', but we too may be easily overawed by stimuli around us. We are likely to respond to the most forceful rather than the most significant. Even when working with an individual child we may become so overwhelmed with our own thoughts and predictions about what we expect to see, based on our expectations, that we may miss what is actually there.

Parents' needs

It is important to acknowledge what parents of children with SLCN need from the practitioners who work with their children. While the following list applies to all parents, these needs are particularly relevant to parents of children with communication difficulties.

Parents need:

- to have their child noticed;
- to have their intuitive skills recognised;
- to know that their interaction with their child is important;
- to have a shared vocabulary with the practitioners supporting their child;
- to be able to share the excitement of any developmental changes;
- to be helped within a supportive setting to see their child's skills in a positive light;
- to know what to support in their child's development;
- to know how to provide useful feedback.

Doing it together

If practitioners are able to spend at least five minutes daily of special dedicated time with individual children with SLCN, responding to their specific needs, then it is likely that some change in their communication may be affected. Spending such time will enable practitioners to help children learn at their own pace, and will support them in developing their own skills. This will possibly be even more effective if it is done in close consultation with the parents and with the support and collaboration of a speech and language therapist.

Daily special dedicated time – five minutes a day

This special time should take place in a 'personal, cosy space'. This is the time when noise should be kept to a minimum so that the child may become completely focussed, engaged in an activity they enjoy. This may be something the parents have said the child likes to do, or something the child has been observed enjoying in the early years setting such as playing in the water tray, the sand box, or in the playhouse outside. Engagement in such activities may help the child to understand that there are situations where it is appropriate to be focussed without having to speak.

At such times it is important to be able to form an attachment with the child so that s/he might feel safe, because it is very important that the child is in control of the communication.

Reading the signals

Eye contact and 'body watching'

Reading body language, 'body watching', involves observing the signals on people's faces and interpreting their demeanour from them as well as from their posture and movements (see Chapter 1).

However, children with SLCN do not always appear to watch other people's faces. They may look at someone, or watch from a distance, but they rarely use eye contact to start an interaction, for example.

Children without communication difficulties will approach adults, look at them directly, say something, listen to the response and then look away to signal that the interaction is over. When they turn their eyes away or look down, the adult usually stops speaking, watching the child's face and gaze aversion as a cue to lower the level of their behaviour (Stern 2002). It may well be that children with SLCN stop using their eyes to initiate a conversation because the adults do not appear to be taking notice of their specific non-verbal signal. As the adults try to compensate for the children's difficulties they over-ride the eye signals and continue to talk/question. Then the message to the children is that their eye contact has not affected the adult's behaviour, so they discontinue using it.

Developing the confident use of eye contact is a gradual process that may be developed during periods of 'daily special dedicated time'. The consistency of the response of the adult will contribute to the success of the development of eye contact, for example by showing that they are comfortable with silence. There is a marked difference between the adult making the child look and waiting for the child to choose to look. The adult should not ask the child to look or place any pressure on the child to look; the object is for the child to initiate/choose the contact.

Face watching is part of the behaviour of all new babies and their parents, regardless of their culture (Aitkin and Trevarthan 1997), and is part of the non-verbal behaviour underpinning language development. After developing face-watching abilities children then learn to use eye contact in a way that is in keeping with their own family's cultural mores, which will be modelled by their family.

Proximity

As the child settles in to their special dedicated time, doing what they like to do, it is important for the adult to place themselves opposite the child. They need to be in natural proximity so that the child can feel that the adult is attentive, interested and ready should they wish to engage.

Silence and Time

The daily special dedicated time is not about how the adult is able to engage the child or how the adult can get the child to respond. It is a quiet time in which all demands for the child to communicate or talk are removed so that they can choose to initiate interaction if they wish.

What the process is about

- Providing an opportunity for silence. The child needs to know that it is all right to do something in an adult's presence without having to engage.
- Inhibiting the adult's own need to compensate and take over.
- Reducing extraneous distractions. This allows the child to focus their full attention on what they wish to do.
- Giving the child time to self-regulate and calm their emotional state. This will influence their developing attention and listening skills and encourage positive behaviour.
- Giving the child time to explore and experiment, the pre-cursers to language, while knowing they have the adult's undivided attention.
- Letting the child have control over what they are doing, and allowing them time to organise themselves.
- Making the time relevant and meaningful because it is the child's focus. It should also be memorable as it will be giving them pleasure.
- Giving them time to co-ordinate their body, their posture, their fine and gross motor movements, and their thoughts.
- Providing processing time commensurate with their current stage of development.

- Showing them trust and interest and providing a model of waiting and listening.
- Allowing them to choose to engage and to initiate communication with their eyes.

In this dedicated time the child is provided with the opportunity to explore, experiment and sequence their ideas and thoughts. It allows them time in a supported environment for enjoyment through physical exploration.

The adult is waiting for eye contact from the child as the trigger for when they can speak. If the child looks at them, however briefly, then that is the signal for the adult to nod affirmation and say a word about what the child is doing, such as 'pouring' or 'boo'.

While the adult waits for eye contact it allows time for the child to develop their ability to watch people's faces, and to get feedback and information about the other person's emotions and feelings. It allows the child to have control, giving them a chance to self-regulate and calm themselves. It offers them the opportunity to control the rate and pace of the interaction and the timing of turn-taking. By looking away the child is able to stop the adult talking. This provides the child with invaluable processing time in which to organise and process their own thoughts and intentions.

At the same time the adult learns to recognise when the child is ready to engage. They stop speaking when the child looks away and only speak when the child looks to them to do so. In this way the adult provides words when the child seeks them and provides the child with silence and processing time when necessary.

Each positive response to the eye contact, either a smile or a word, will encourage the child who will want to engage more in this way. When we make eye contact we look at someone's face and we often automatically mirror the other's facial expression. The child therefore will receive reinforcement both non-verbally and verbally. The child will then look away and the adult will return to silence.

When the child eventually looks again at the adult, the word spoken will literally shatter the silence, making it distinctive and salient from all other surrounding sound. Now that the child is face-watching they are helped to focus on the relevant details of the adult's facial expression – their lip patterns, and the salient aspects of the sounds – and it is all occurring at the child's own pace. The beginnings and ends of the words – the word boundaries – are clear and the child sees the shape of the word on the adult's lips. The child also sees the adult's facial expression accompanying the word. In this way the child sees and hears the word within context and with meaning; and it is all within the child's control – it is self-regulating, for the child does not look up if they wish to block out the words.

With each session consistency of opportunity is important. The child's eye contact and consistency of face-watching is likely to increase as they see the impact they are able to have on the interaction. They will begin to seek more words and meaning for what they are doing. Their attention and concentration naturally develops as they are given time to focus and explore, to succeed and make an impact. With each session the nature of their eye contact will also develop.

The development of eye contact and face watching

- In the early stages children may just 'chin watch' – glance to see if the adult will speak and look away to see if the adult will stop speaking.
- They will start to hold the adult's face in view for longer and watch them say the whole word once they are confidently able to predict that the speaking will stop when they look away.
- They will start to mirror the adult's facial expression, which will have been a smile accompanying the spoken word.
- They will start to watch the adult's lips and be attentive to what is being said.
- They will start to 'repair' if the adult chooses the wrong word and watch the adult's face to see how they adjust.
- They will start to watch the adult's face for signs of feedback.

What we as practitioners are monitoring is how the child's ability to face watch and make eye contact is emerging. We will automatically provide the child with what they need linguistically if we are able to watch, listen and respond according to whatever developmental stage they are at.

Different developmental stages

- If they look and have few words – we will name the object in their hand or the action they are doing, such as 'cup' or 'drinking'.
- If they vocalise but the sound they make is not specific, for example 'uga', we will recast what we have heard into the relevant, recognisable word, 'cup'.
- If they say a single word, 'tea', we nod and add additional words such as '**he's drinking** tea'.
- If their utterance is not accurate, 'man run', we nod and recast the sentence, stressing the additional words which they have omitted, '**the man is running**'.
- If they are using lengthy utterances which are unclear, 'Daddy went dopping on de but', we wait for them to make eye contact, smile, slow our rate of speech and stress the elements of the word they were not saying clearly, 'Oh, he went **shopping** on the **bus**'.
- Or if the child uses a lengthy utterance but is dysfluent (see Chapter 6), we wait for eye contact, slow our own rate and respond at a measured rate.

We are highlighting the elements that we want the child to pay attention to at an appropriate time and in an appropriate communicative situation. These recasts are stretching the child to the next stage of their development through the 'zone of proximal development' (Vygotsky 1962).

If required, in addition we can supplement the words we speak with some kind of augmentative system of communication, such as a sign or a symbol.

Feedback for parents

In this situation it is we – the practitioners/adults – who are the 'students', learning about the specific interaction timing. At the same time we are carefully observing the child's emerging skills. We are training ourselves to focus on new levels of detail, although this may sometimes be difficult to see. Within the context of daily life the emerging signals may well be overshadowed. It would be helpful therefore if some of the daily special dedicated sessions could be recorded and analysed with the help of a speech and language therapist, as many of the child's early signals are so subtle that they may well be missed without the support of 'freeze frame'. This would enable us to look back at the recording and see:

- when we are meeting the child's gaze;
- when we are moderating our own speech;
- each step of the child's development;
- how the child is able to control the interaction with their eyes.

Even more importantly, we can share the recording with the parents and explain what is happening in terms of the development of the child's increasing confidence in initiating and participating in play and interaction. This record will provide a baseline measure, with specific evidence, of the child's communication level at the outset of the daily dedicated sessions in terms of their communication skills: self-regulation; attention; listening; eye contact and face watching; communicative intent; comprehension; and expression. It will also provide evidence for the outcomes of how the child is developing week by week.

The parents may then choose to explore similar scenarios at home, integrating the concepts into action songs, bath time, time on the swings in the park, or story times. They may wish to film themselves during their special dedicated times at home and bring in the recordings for discussion.

By experimenting, experiencing, thinking, reflecting and acting together we are able to discuss a range of relevant issues such as the child's increasing attention span, improving behaviour and increasing interests and explorations. Practitioners and parents will then have a shared vocabulary and a greater clarity about what they are doing and why. We become joint researchers in the child's development.

A recording may be particularly helpful with parents for whom English is an additional language and who may be communicating with the practitioner through a third party. By sharing the recording through an interpreter, advocate or friend we can explore what it means for the family, and highlight the universal principles of focusing on eye contact and face watching while observing the parent naming, repeating, recasting and extending in the language most pertinent to the child.

Integrating

The child's communicative intent and role in interaction will begin to be evident within the general early years environment. Having developed eye contact and face-watching skills with their parents and with early years practitioners, the child will begin to experiment using it with their peers and other practitioners, for example when they are part of a group where they feel equal to their peers. Similarly they will be able to access the wide variety of language enrichment activities available to them with increasing confidence.

We can facilitate the child's success by gradually introducing other children into the working sessions – at first a pair and then a small group. The group may include typically developing children who may also be able to support the child with SLCN. Parents may be able to observe or participate in these groups and watch their child's skills emerging.

Collaboration

When managing children's development it is necessary for parents and practitioners to be:

- congruent
- consistent
- predictable
- reliable.

This is not only with the child, but also with each other, within the team and with members of other agencies.

We as practitioners need to reflect on our collaboration skills, for example when working together with the professional team. We need to be able to share information and strategies specific to each child, and we need to have a shared ethos and sense of purpose such as dedicated times allocated for working with targeted special children.

All early years practitioners need to reflect on their collaboration with other agencies, particularly with speech and language therapists, in terms of accessibility and shared working practice. The best way of doing this is through video reflection. We need to share ideas and information, and ensure we have effective systems for liaison.

Parents may be able to use video examples of their child's emerging skills in meetings with other agencies such as psychologists, occupational therapists, speech and language therapists and/or physiotherapists. They may be able to integrate any additional advice and strategies that might be suggested.

Parental support

It is also important that parents have access to communities that have experience of the issues they are facing. This may be arranged within the early years setting or locally. Parent groups are usually able to provide a great deal of detailed knowledge as well as emotional support. Many parent groups take the initiative in putting people in touch with others and establishing support for their peers. Social media provides access to a host of specific networks which may also provide support. The stronger the relationship between practitioners and parents, the more they are able to share mutually supportive initiatives and ideas.

Workshops and peer participation

Parents may wish to attend organised workshops in which they have the opportunity to discuss and reflect on certain topics such as indoor and outdoor exploration and play, the benefits of visual support, for example through action songs, Makaton, books and nursery rhymes, or managing the environment.

Conclusion

The more open we as practitioners are to incorporating and using the skills and creativity of the parents of the children with whom we work, the more we stand to gain both professionally and personally. Parents may become more confident if we ensure that we make the most of their skills, knowledge and understanding so that we all fully understand the reasoning behind the principles guiding our collaborative work. Parents will then be in a stronger position to influence the child's communicative environment and the child's developing skills, and to inform others about how they also might support their child's development.

References

Aitken, K.J. and Trevarthen, C. (1997) Self/other organization in human psychological development. *Development and Psychopathology*, 9, 653–677.

Cummins, K. and Hulme, S. (2001) Managing pre-school children in community clinics. In M. Kersner and J.A. Wright (Eds.), *Speech and Language Therapy: the decision-making process when working with children*. London: David Fulton Publishers.

Rogers, C. (1951) *Client-centred Therapy: Its current practice, implications and theory*. London: Constable.

Royal College of Speech and Language Therapists (2006) *Communicating Quality 3*. London: RCSLT.

Schon, D. (1983) *The Reflective Practitioner*. London: Maurice Temple Smith Basic Books.

Stern, D. (2002) *The First Relationship, Infant and Mother*. Boston: Harvard University Press.

Vygotsky, L. (1962) *Thought and Language*. Boston: MIT Press.

Further reading

Early Years Foundation Stage Handbook Product code STA/14/7088/e, PDF version ISBN: 978-1-78315-324-4. www.gov.uk/government/publications/early-years-foundation-stage-profile-handbook-2014eyeyfs

Gerhardt, S. (2004) *Why Love Matters: How affection shapes a baby's brain*. London: Routledge.

Pound, L. (2005) *How Children Learn from Montessori to Vygotsky: Educational theories and approaches made easy*. London: Step Forward Publishing Ltd.

Weitzman, E. and Greenberg, J. (2008) (2nd edition) *Learning Language and Loving It*. Toronto: The Hanen Centre.

Chapter 6

Stammering and early dysfluency in young children

Trudy Stewart and Alison McLaughlin

Introduction

In this chapter we will consider many of the questions and concerns which often face parents of children who start to stammer. The issue of stammering can be a difficult one to address. One of the authors has personal experience of being a parent of a child who had a period of dysfluency, so we have some understanding of the emotional reaction that can take place. We hope that this chapter will enable parents and other professionals to understand the factors that are important and to know when to seek help from a speech and language therapist.

What is stammering?

'My child doesn't have a stammer, but he does get stuck on his words and stutters sometimes.'

The words 'stammering' and 'stuttering' are terms that are frequently used to describe the same complex behaviour. 'Stuttering' is largely used outside of the UK, but 'stammering' and 'dysfluency' are more commonly used in the UK and so for consistency these terms will be used throughout this chapter. It can be confusing for parents when they are trying to make sense of, and to describe, changes that they have noticed in their child's speech. We have often found that children, parents and professionals do not find these terms particularly helpful, and nor do they contribute to their understanding of stammering. However, asking a child to describe his own speech can provide a shared understanding of what stammering means for the individual child and make an excellent starting point for anyone working with him.

When Joey and his parents visited our clinic it was the first time they had spoken openly about his stammer. Joey found it difficult to describe what happened to his speech in words, but he was able to show us; he demonstrated a stop-start walk across the room. During this walk he would send himself

back to the beginning and at times flailed his arms in the air uncontrollably.
Joey said this was how his talking felt, and he called it 'hibberty bobbity'.
This demonstration enabled Joey and his parents to have a shared
understanding of his experience and they were all able to use a term that was
meaningful from that point forward.

Stammering has been described and documented for centuries, and it continues to be found in all populations throughout the world. Despite this, there is no clear and universally accepted definition of stammering. For years, people who stammer, speech and language therapists and researchers have been trying to understand the processes that lead to the incoordination of articulation affecting the flow and timing of speech.

Learning to talk is complicated and it is quite usual for children to stumble over words, hesitate, and stop and start again. Early stammering usually begins between the ages of two and four years and is more common in boys than girls.

Stammering is often seen at a time when a child's speech and language skills are rapidly expanding, though for some it can start on or near the development of their first words. Its appearance can be both sudden and severe, but this initial pattern does not mean a child will go on to stammer in later years. During this normal developmental stage it can be difficult to decide whether the disruption to speech flow and timing is 'normal', i.e. an exaggeration of typical disruptions seen in most speech, or if it is early stammering.

The good news is that most children will grow out of, or spontaneously recover from, stammering. Research has shown that recovery may be as high as seventy-five per cent of children, and this recovery is likely to happen within the first two years of onset. However, research suggests that the longer a child has been stammering the greater the risk of persistence, and this is particularly true of girls. So if a child has been experiencing a consistent level of disruption for six months or longer it is recommended that the family see a speech and language therapist to have it checked out.

There is a significant amount that speech and language therapists now understand about stammering, but every child is different. When the door opens and a child and their family walk into a speech and language therapy clinic their history, experience, expectations and the process of learning and growing together is unique. It is this uniqueness that is both interesting and challenging when trying to make sense of each child's stammering.

A speech and language therapist will spend a lot of time exploring the child's speech, and she will talk to him and his family about their concerns. One thing a specialist speech and language therapist may do is analyse his speech and look for features that could indicate the risk of persistent stammering.

Normal non-fluency

Take a look at the following examples. The question being asked is the same, but there are some key features that can help us to identify stammering:

> *Mum ... can I have ... can I have ... you know ... a biscuit?*

This is an example of normal non-fluency. Even as adults we can experience hesitation or false starts. In fact these dysfluencies can be seen in all speakers, especially if they are tired, excited or not fully concentrating on what they are saying. However, there is something distinctly different in stammered speech that helps us to distinguish it from normal non-fluency.

> *M..m..m..mummy caaaaan I I I have a bis bis bis biscuit?*

This example is of more concern, as the child has begun to fragment words into segments. A therapist would be interested in any increase in the speed and number of repetitions heard on a sound or word, as research has shown this to be important. There may also be elements of tension or struggle seen in a child's face or body movements, such as hand tapping or head movement. This tension may also be heard if sounds become stretched out or become stuck and no sound is heard. Unusual breathing patterns may also be observed. We have seen children who take in quick breaths before speaking, or who appear to be running out of breath. Children can experience some or all of these changes in their speech and non-speech behaviours when stammering begins.

Their reaction to this change can also vary from child to child. Some parents report that their child is aware of stammering as soon as it starts. This awareness can be seen before, during or after the moment of stammering, and a child may ask '*Why can't I say it?*' and show concern in some way – for example, their face becomes flushed. However, other children will show no anticipation or awareness of stammering.

It is not enough to understand a child's difficulty by simply describing a list of speech behaviours that can be seen or heard. To appreciate the whole picture we also need to consider how a child is experiencing and making sense of their stammering. We will talk in detail about how stammering develops, including emotional, psychological and cognitive issues, throughout this chapter.

'Myth busting'

Families, other professionals and children who stammer often have their own theory of what causes stammering. In this section we will describe some of these beliefs and, where appropriate, look at the evidence to support them.

Myth: A child can develop stammering by imitation

'He sits next to a little boy in his class who stammers. Is he copying him?'

Stammering behaviour can be copied in the same way that you might mimic an accent. However, it would be difficult for a young child to maintain this behaviour, and it is somewhat curious to consider why a child might want to do this for a long period of time.

Myth: Parents think they are responsible for their child's stammer

'Is it our fault?'

No, parents do not cause stammering. Parents can feel responsible and experience feelings of guilt, helplessness and blame. In fact, they play a crucial role in working out how and why their child is stammering. A parent's perception of stammering and how they react to their child's dysfluency is highly significant. They are best placed to support or modify a child's environment and provide him with a positive role model. The part played by parents has become integral to some interventions used with children who stammer, such as the Palin Parent–Child Interaction Approach (Kelman and Nicholas 2008) and the Lidcome Programme of Early Stuttering Intervention (Onslow et al. 2003). We would always advocate working closely with parents and involving them in all aspects of their child's therapy.

Myth: Stammering is caused by being anxious

'I don't understand, it can happen at any time – do you think it's because she's a nervous person?'

People often associate stammering with being nervous or anxious. This is a common misconception, possibly because behaviours like stammering can be experienced by fluent speakers at times when they feel nervous or anxious. Someone who stammers is actually no more nervous or anxious than an individual who does not stammer. Research has shown that, as a group, there is no difference in levels of confidence, anxiety or nervousness among people who stammer when compared to others.

However, while it might not cause stammering, anxiety may play a part. Anxiety is acknowledged to be an emotional response associated with stammering. We know that as time goes by children, young people and adults experience anticipation of stammering prior to speaking situations, and thus they may also anticipate negative consequences.

Myth: Stammering is caused by specific food

'I gave him some Brazil nuts and after that he started to stammer.'

There is little research on links between the onset or development of stammering and what children eat. Some foods and drinks have been reported to affect attention levels and can be physiologically stimulating. However, we have no reliable information on the relationship between stammering and nutrition.

Myth: Stammering is caused by trauma

'It started when our dog died. He was so upset, they were always together; I think losing him really affected him.'

It is not unusual to hear parents talking about significant or traumatic events that they associate with the onset of stammering. While for most children the event itself will not cause a stammer to develop, it may coincide with other significant events or stages of a child's development. The experience of trauma for the child at risk of developing a persistent stammer can appear to be what tips an already vulnerable scale.

In the following section we will look at what makes a child more vulnerable to stammering by considering both current research and what we have noticed about children we have seen in our clinics.

Current theories

One of the most frequently asked questions is *'What causes stammering?'* Stammering is a complex disorder of speech and communication and identifying a single cause is unlikely. However, the last decade has seen the greatest advances in our understanding of stammering. Historically the view taken to understand stammering was one-dimensional. We now acknowledge that it is likely to be related to several factors and we need to view it in a multidimensional way.

The most useful way to understand stammering is from an individual's perspective. It is crucial to hear the child describe his experience and listen to parents share what they have noticed about their child. We can then begin to develop a hypothesis about why stammering has started, and crucially whether the child may be at risk of stammering into adulthood. Being able to identify risk is key to knowing at the earliest possible time which child needs help.

Key factors

The following sections need to be considered as pieces of a jigsaw. Understanding stammering in this way can help build a profile of what makes a child more vulnerable to persistent, long-term stammering.

Family history

Ella's father and grandfather both stammered. Ella's father shared his concerns that she would stammer like him and wanted to do everything he could to support her, as he had never felt able to discuss his stammer at home with his father.

There is strong evidence showing an increased risk of a child stammering if there is a close family member who currently stammers. In addition, if that family member has recovered from stammering later in life, then the child is more likely to inherit this pattern of recovery.

This risk for developing stammering is higher for boys than girls. Pioneering research is being carried out to identify specific genes associated with stammering. Genealogy can help us identify children who are at risk of stammering, but current thinking also acknowledges the role played by the child's environment. Thus, the interplay of genetics (internal) and the environment (external) needs to be understood in each child.

We often meet parents who stammer, and some have shared with us their sense of responsibility for their child's stammer. We encourage those parents to have a stance of openness and to try to develop an understanding of the child's experience of stammering. This is particularly helpful for a child who may go on to stammer in the long term. Talking with your child about your own experiences can reduce feelings of isolation and any concerns about being the 'only one'. Creating an environment that is open to talking about stammering can be empowering for both the parent and the child.

Brain functions

During a parent workshop one parent said she felt worried, as she had heard there was something wrong with the brains of people who stammer. The rest of the group were surprised to hear this and wanted to understand more about it.

Recent advances in the use of brain imaging have allowed us to make some important observations of both the structure and function of the brains of individuals who stammer. These images have indicated that key areas of the brain, crucial in language production, respond and react differently in those who stammer. The research indicates some differences in the development of neural pathways in the brain. These pathways continue to develop in childhood and this may go some way to explain why stammering appears and then stops in some children as neural pathways develop.

This does not mean that there is anything 'wrong' with the brain of a child who stammers. In fact, imaging has also shown how children who stammer can adapt and find alternative pathways using other parts of the brain.

It is important that parents seek support from a speech and language therapist as early as possible so that a full assessment can be carried out and the appropriate treatment can begin.

Links with language skills

At a school visit, Sally's teacher shared with the speech and language therapist that she was puzzled by how Sally performed in classroom discussions. 'It just seems like she can't get her head round what she wants to say.'

There is evidence to suggest that language is one of the factors involved in stammering in children. Children who stammer often have additional speech and language difficulty, such as poorer speech sounds skills (phonology). Both advanced and low language levels can exacerbate stammering, as can problems with language processing. Language skills alone are not the most reliable predictor for persistence, but they do need to be considered. A specialist speech and language therapist can carry out a full assessment to rule out any delay or mismatches in a child's speech and language profile and to consider the impact this may have on the type, place and severity of stammering.

Bilingualism and stammering

Mikael and his family had recently moved from Poland. During his Reception year at school his parents and his teachers noticed that he had started to stammer. At home his parents only used the Polish language but at school he was exposed to and was encouraged to use English.

There is not enough known about the relationship between stammering and bi/multilingualism. There is evidence to suggest that stammering is higher in children who speak more than one language. Being bi/multilingual may also have an impact on language development in some children. Speech and language therapists try and establish the level of dysfluency in each language spoken. They would consider whether or not this difficulty relates to the learning of two or more languages or to the timing of the introduction of an additional language.

Personality

Will began stammering when he was in Reception. His parents described him as a 'worrier' and as someone who didn't like change. They had noticed that even as a toddler he liked to get things right and would get frustrated easily. If he could not get a piece to fit into a puzzle he would get upset and throw it across the floor. Mum said, 'He always likes to get things right; he's just like me really.'

Parents often describe their child as sensitive, impulsive, easily upset or finding change in routine difficult. As a group, children who stammer appear to be more reactive to outside events or situations. They also appear less able to regulate or control these responses. A reactive personality is not the cause of stammering, but it can lead to a child being less able to tolerate dysfluent speech over time.

Environment

Finley came to the centre at the age of two years five months. His language was advanced for his age; he was using wide vocabulary and putting together long and complex sentences. At home he lived with two older sisters and his mother had just had another baby. The house was described by mum as 'chaos' and 'loud', and everyone was vying for space and attention.

A lot has been written about the influence of a child's environment and stammering. For parents and professionals it can be helpful to look together at what may be having an impact on a child's ability to speak with flow and ease. Consider a set of weighing scales; an even amount on each side of the scale is required to maintain balance. Let's apply this to speaking; a chaotic home and a constant battle to get his parents' attention could be seen as a demand on Finley's capacity to be fluent. Finley's parents identified that he may experience a sense of urgency and competition with his older and younger siblings and a need to communicate concisely in order to be heard. These demands led to the breakdown of his fluency – that is, stammering.

When we talk to parents about ways in which they can help it is often small changes in this area that can have the biggest impact on their child's level of dysfluency. For Finley, introducing 'Special Time', five minutes of one-to-one time with his parents away from the other children, gave him the experience of speaking without the time pressure and the competition created by others. By making this change his parents could see the impact that reducing demands on his speech could have on his stammering.

None of the factors discussed in this section should be considered in isolation. In the same way, the environment should not be seen as the only demand that can affect a child's fluency level. A specialist speech and language therapist will spend some time identifying a child's individual demands and capacities for speech. Together parents and professionals can look at how a balance can be achieved. In addition, it is important to understand how stammering can develop over time.

How stammering develops

At the age of three Kyle suddenly started stammering. It seemed to come from nowhere. One day he was speaking without difficulties and the next day he was struggling to get his words out. He would try to say the first word and be unable to move off the first sound; sometimes he would repeat the sound several times and other times he would stretch it for a few seconds before finally pushing it out with great effort. It came as a shock to his parents who tried to find reasons as to why it had suddenly appeared; was he unwell, or had he been upset by something? However, it was much more of a shock to Kyle whose behaviour became more aggressive, his moods more variable and he began to wet the bed.

Brian began stammering also when he was around three and a half but it began in a different way. Brian experienced a much more gradual onset; in fact, his parents hardly noticed it had begun. Then it dawned on them one day that he was having difficulty getting started, quite often when he wanted to ask them something. Subsequently they noticed that Brian's stammering was more noticeable at different times. At several points his parents thought it had disappeared altogether and then it came back for no apparent reason. The variability meant that they were unable to relax during the fluent phases. They and Brian were always waiting for it to reappear.

These two examples illustrate clearly that there is not one way in which stammering develops. There can be many different presentations, some of which may be more significant than others.

Let us consider some background to the development of stammering in children. Joseph Sheehan, an American speech and language pathologist, was the first person to talk about stammering using the metaphor of an iceberg. Sheehan (1958) used the iceberg to describe stammering because of its structure; an observable or overt part above the water line and a hidden or covert part, often much larger, underneath.

In stammering terms, the overt part consists of what listeners see and hear; the repetitions of sounds and syllables, the prolongations or stretching of sounds, disrupted breathing patterns and perhaps some associated struggling behaviour such as facial grimacing, jaw jerks or arm and leg movements. On the other hand, the covert components of stammering would be unobservable to the untrained listener and consist of avoidance behaviours such as avoiding certain words or situations due to the fear of stammering, and the emotional and psychological responses of the speaker to his stammering. Examples of this might be negative thoughts such as *'This person is going to think I am stupid because I stammer'*, or negative feelings such as shame, guilt, anger or frustration.

If we apply this information to the development of stammering, it is clear that it would be rare for young children to have a covert component to their stammering from its onset. More typically, at the start and in the early stages a child would have a totally overt stammer; what we observe a young child doing is all of his stammer. This is a great place to be, and one that would be likely to yield a positive outcome. It is much easier to treat and manage stammering speech that is not complicated by unhelpful thoughts and feelings. In this situation control and different speaking techniques can then focus on learning new behaviours or skills, like adopting a new way of walking, riding a bike or learning to swim.

With Jack, we discovered that his stammering was linked to his need to have time to find the words he wished to say and construct his sentences. Once that was understood, those around him gave him more planning time and modelled a slower paced use of language. Jack soon adopted this for himself and relaxed more when thinking about what he had to say. As a result he became more fluent.

Unfortunately covert stammering behaviours can develop over time. This may come about due to the influence of peers or through the development of the child's self-awareness. Consequently, he becomes aware that stammering speech is not acceptable and needs to be changed and avoided if at all possible. Sometimes he learns that stammering happens on certain words, so he will avoid saying that word and substitute it for another. Sometimes a child learns that stammering happens at specific times, such as when talking in front of a group or asking the teacher a question in class. So then he makes a choice not to do those things to avoid stammering. 'Show and tell' may become a child's worst activity rather than an opportunity to share a joyous experience or impress his peers.

Consider the following: a child who chooses not to ask his teacher questions could fail to learn and compromise his academic achievement in the long term. Indeed, the word compromise is significant when we think about the development of covert components in stammering. If not checked, negative thoughts and feelings, and avoidances of speaking, can result in an individual who lives a compromised life – not choosing the academic subjects in which he has particular abilities because they involve too much speaking, not establishing significant relationships in later life because 'that certain someone' will find out about his stammering, not being the person he truly is because of stammering.

Some of the most significant examples of this are the children who choose not to speak because of the fear of being judged or ridiculed because of their speech difficulties.

Oliver said so little in school he was thought of as shy, lacking in confidence and with low average abilities. In fact, once the school were made aware of his speech issues and made reasonable adjustments to classroom interactions, he became more engaged with the lesson material, a more active contributor and his academic performance improved considerably.

Thus the key issues in the development of stammering in children are:

- the appearance of stammering speech and its early identification;
- the reaction of the child, or others, to this type of talking;
- the subsequent development of negative thoughts and feelings and avoidance behaviours;
- the choice of the child to compromise who they are because of their stammering.

How parents can help

Below are some ideas and practical suggestions for how to minimise the impact of stammering, with a specific focus on the covert component of stammering.

Mustafa is eleven and has stammered since he was four. His parents are very worried because he is soon to start secondary school. His dad has concerns about Mustafa's ability to achieve high grades in all subjects, especially those which involve speaking in class. His mother is also worried that he may be bullied about his talking and be without friends. Their worries lead them to remind Mustafa to talk fluently when he speaks to them.

Maired has quite a noticeable stammer. She repeats sounds almost on every sentence and often gets stuck on vowels at the beginning of words. Her mother gets upset when Maired stammers in this way. She remembers her own father stammering when he spoke and how it upset him. She does not ever talk about how she feels to Maired, but instead tries to talk for her when people ask her direct questions. She tries hard to make Maired happy and will often buy her toys and sweets.

These two examples illustrate how individual parents can react in different ways to their child's stammering. Parenting is hard at the best of times and it is made even more complex when your child has specific needs that must be managed. All parents ever want is to do the best for their child, but knowing just what to do can be very difficult.

Hearing your child stammering can evoke lots of negative emotions: anxiety or panic that this is going to affect his life; guilt or shame that in some way you are responsible, even anger that it has come about and a desire to blame someone for it. If you experience these emotions it is important to remember that parents do not cause stammering. Indeed, parents can be part of the solution and integral to the effective management of stammering in children. So what should you do? It is difficult to give some specific rules that will apply to the parent of every child who stammers, but below are some suggested starting points.

Value your child for what he is, not for how you would like him to be

Each child has his own strengths and weaknesses. You may wish your child was better at certain things than others, but he is a wonderful individual with potential to make his own particular mark on society. You need to celebrate exactly who he is, rather than who he could be if he just did something else or tried harder.

Establish an open relationship

Every child needs to know that his parents are there when he needs support. All parents need to establish open communication so that when the child wants to talk he knows the parent will respond positively. For some children it can be hard to be open and vulnerable with others. Parents can be great role models in this regard, talking about some of their own difficulties and how they manage them.

Alyia was quite anxious about starting a new class. Her mother told her stories from her own experience about going into new situations and how she managed her own anxieties, for example talking to someone about it beforehand or finding someone to go into the difficult situation with.

Listen, listen, listen

There is a difference between casual and active listening. When we are actively listening we are completely focussed on the speaker; we would not be engaged in any other activity, we would be looking at them, concentrating on what they were telling us, and unaware of our own thoughts and feelings. Active listening is essential when communicating with children, especially those with problems expressing their ideas. Consider for a moment how a rabbit listens, as an animal who relies on his senses to survive. A rabbit will stop, be still in his body, attune to his environment and use his senses to understand what is being presented to him. Curious though this may be, we can learn from this.

Suggestions for good listening

- Stop what you are doing. If you cannot do that, then tell the child when you will be able to listen.
- Look at the child using soft eye contact, not staring.
- Suspend what is on your mind and concentrate on the content of what the child is saying.
- Do not judge, belittle or in any way invalidate what the child says by making comments like, 'Oh it's not as bad as that', or 'I'm sure he didn't mean it'.
- Ask questions to make sure you fully understand what the child is trying to communicate.
- Finally, summarise what you think the child has said. This will demonstrate to the child that he has been listened to and that you have understood.

Stand in the child's shoes

Another way of saying this is to be empathetic. The word empathy means 'feeling into' – feeling into the child's experience, his emotion, thoughts and behaviours. It can be difficult to set aside your own experience, your own evaluation of situations and adopt the child's perspective. If you do not do this, however, then the child will not feel validated and understood. To be able to truly 'stand in the shoes' of a child you need to make sure your awareness is the same as theirs. A younger child may have little or no awareness of speech difficulties, whereas a teenager may be acutely aware and be performing all manner of verbal gymnastics to avoid stammering overtly.

Focus on the positives

His speech might be less than perfect, but there are sure to be other areas of the child's life which are worthy of praise. Helping a child to notice the things that are going well and making him feel supported can enable him to value himself for what he is.

Zain struggled to talk in class but he was great at drawing. His mum told him she really liked his drawings of animals and encouraged him to draw some pictures of his visit to the zoo. He took them into school and used them to help him tell his class mates about his exciting trip.

Further suggestions for how to communicate with a child who stammers

- *Reduce 'demand' speech* For example, instead of saying 'Your auntie is on the phone. Tell her about your visit to the zoo at the weekend', try to give him a choice about what he might talk about, who he might speak to and when he might speak – by saying, for example, 'I am going to talk to your auntie on the phone. I wonder if there is anything you would like to talk to her about?'

- *Use a slower rate of speech* Some children who stammer do so because they need a longer time to process their sentences, and stammering is a way of getting that extra time. If the person to whom they are speaking is using a slow speaking rate, then the child will subconsciously feel he has longer to work out what he wants to say and will not rush his processing.

- *Encourage turn taking* A child who stammers often worries that someone is going to 'steal' his talking turn by saying his words for him, interrupting or talking over his dysfluent words. This may give him the message that, for some reason, the utterance is less important because the words are stammered. By establishing clear rules of communication in a family, including one that values each and everyone's talking turn, the child will feel less anxious about the possibility of losing his turn.

- *Consider giving advice* Parents want to help a child whose speech is dysfluent and in some way 'make it better'. As discussed in the earlier section, it is important to understand what is at the heart of the stammer in order to give the right response. Is it the result of a language processing problem? Or are there difficulties in the dynamics of a particular situation which create significant demands on the child's communication? Seeing a speech and language therapist, especially one who specialises in stammering, will help you find out what the issues might be and therefore what is the best advice you can give your child.

We recommend visiting a speech and language therapist as soon as you have concerns and getting advice early. Research indicates that early intervention can be effective in helping a child gain fluency and develop strategies to manage a stammer should it persist.

Recommendations for other professionals involved with the child

Children spend a good proportion of their days with educators in various settings. These may include early years settings or school and those leisure activities which involve learning, such as swimming, football, dance classes, singing groups, Rainbows, Beavers and Brownies. It is important that all those working with a child who stammers use the same principles as those listed above.

In addition, there are specific activities which may be problematic and therefore warrant special advice.

- *Responding to the register* Saying your name in front of a group of peers within a set time frame is one of those high demand situations, i.e. saying a specific thing to a specific person or set of people at a set time. A child who is experiencing dysfluent speech needs to be given choices: the choice of what to say and how he can respond; the choice of when he can say the response; and plenty of time in which to say it. He also needs to be confident that, should he overtly stammer, the situation will be managed sensitively, with any reactions from others dealt with appropriately. In addition, if the register is done in a particular order, it would be helpful if this is modified to enable the child who is dysfluent to speak early in the order, perhaps second or third in the list.
- *Questions and answers* Direct questions and specific answers also fall in the category of high demand situations. Being chosen at random to answer a quick question or always having to ask questions to clarify information in front of others can be difficult for a child experiencing stammering. Allowing the child to choose when he answers and what questions he responds to is the key to giving him the confidence to try.
- *Reading aloud* Some children find reading aloud easier than spontaneous speech. However, for those children whose dysfluency is related to the fear of saying specific sounds or words, reading can be anticipated with dread. The first thing would be to find out how the child feels about reading aloud in a one-to-one setting and in groups. It may be that he can gain confidence in an individual situation and work up to reading with his peers. Where it is particularly difficult, an adult may pair him up with a trusted friend and have them read in unison as stammering is less likely to happen in this situation.
- *Encouraging contributions* It can be problematic to know how to manage to include a child who stammers in group and performance activities. Children have reported the disappointment of being excluded from an event and the subsequent feeling of not being the same as everyone else. Once again it is important to give the child the choice of what sort of contribution he might make, either a speaking or non-speaking part. If he chooses to speak, then talking to him about the extent of his contribution and what sort of support he might need would be essential.

Summary

In this chapter we have addressed some of the issues we know are important to parents and professionals who work with young children who stammer. We have clarified what stammering is and looked at some of the current theories about its onset and development. We have discussed some of the myths that abound and put them into the context of our knowledge about stammering. We have identified the risks associated with the development of persistent stammering and given some practical suggestions about managing its occurrence in the context of a home or school environment.

References

Kelman, E. and Nicolas, A. (2008) *Practical Intervention for Early Childhood Stammering: Palin PCI approach.* Milton Keynes: Speechmark Publishing Ltd.

Onslow, M., Packman, A. and Harrison, E. (2003) *The Lidcombe Program of Early Stuttering Intervention: A clinician's guide.* Austin, TX: Pro-Ed Inc.

Sheehan, J.G. (1958) Conflict theory and avoidance reduction therapy. In J. Eisenson and O. Bloodstein (Eds.), *Stuttering: A symposium.* Harper: New York.

Further reading

de Geus, E. *Sometimes I Just Stutter,* available from the Stuttering Foundation of America www.stutteringhelp.org/ (a book for children aged 7 to 12).

Holte, D. (2011) (2nd edition) *Voice Unearthed: Hope, help and a wake-up call for the parents of children who stutter.* USA: Holte.

If Your Child Stutters: A guide for parents (8th edition), available from the Stuttering Foundation of America www.stutteringhelp.org/.

Turnbull, J. and Stewart, T. (2010) *Helping Children Cope with Stammering.* London: Sheldon Press.

Chapter 7

Links between social, mental and emotional health difficulties, and communication needs

Melanie Cross

What are social, mental and emotional health difficulties?

In order to understand social, mental and emotional health difficulties (SMEHD) we need to consider mental health. In a warm relationship, initially with parents or carers, children's communication skills grow and their ability to think and understand emotions develops. Using these abilities, they can then build further good relationships with friends and family and develop more skills in language, communicating and understanding other people's feelings and behaviour, all of which contribute to mental health.

Mental health is not about never feeling sad or angry, but about being able to cope with these feelings and being resilient in the face of the difficulties that occur in every child's life. Children who are mentally healthy are also able to use their talents to realise their potential.

The commonest sorts of SMEHD in young children appear as difficulties with sleeping, toileting and eating. Other forms of SMEHD make it hard for children to interact with or learn from others in the usual way. Children who are withdrawn and who have great difficulty in interacting with their peers are a source of considerable concern.

All children are occasionally stressed, shy, sad or angry, but this can usually be managed by the people who care for them. However, some children experience frequent, persistent, extreme emotions and those caring for them can find this very difficult to deal with.

An example of this is children who are much more aggressive than others and who are persistently challenging when children of a similar age are becoming more compliant. Also, some children with SMEHD will be particularly anxious and fearful. Others are very inattentive, restless and impulsive. Children who have experienced traumatic events such as child abuse or neglect might regress in their development, they may show signs of distress when reminded of their experiences, and may show repetitive play or have sleep problems.

How we respond to these difficulties is crucial because early intervention is usually the most effective.

Early indications of long-term difficulties

It is important to be aware of social, mental and emotional health difficulties in young children as they could be the first clues that the child has a long-term developmental difficulty such as speech, language and communication needs (SLCN), Autism Spectrum Disorder (ASD) or Attention Deficit Hyperactivity Disorder (ADHD) which could affect their ability to interact with others, learn and generally progress.

Extreme emotions

Children who experience extreme emotions, or whose emotions stop them doing things children usually do, might need extra support. Similarly, if a child's development is affected or if they are particularly distressed, we should seek help for them. Although specialist help is very important, so are the relationships children have with the people they see every day, and therefore we all need to know how best to help such children manage their emotions and develop their language and communication skills.

It is also essential to work alongside families in order to be as helpful as possible to the child, both in identifying any difficulties and in working together to address them.

Social, mental and emotional health difficulties?

SMEHD can be the result of a variety of factors; there is rarely a single simple 'cause'. Each child's circumstances are different: from their individual temperaments and strengths, to the family they are brought up in, and the stresses they may experience. The most useful thing we can do is to try to understand the numerous influences that could contribute to the difficulties each child is experiencing.

SMEHD is a term introduced in special educational needs legislation to encourage adults to address the underlying needs of a child rather than concentrating on their behaviour.

Risk factors

There are risks and preventative factors for SMEHD. Risk factors in the community or environment include things like socio-economic deprivation and unemployment. This is important as we also know that children from areas of social disadvantage are at increased risk of SLCN (Law et al. 2011). Risk factors in the family include mental health difficulties, an inability to adapt to the child's changing needs, and family conflict. Risk factors within the child might be learning difficulties, SLCN or serious health issues.

Children who are 'looked after' are unfortunately much more likely to have SMEHD than other children.

The role of genetics in SMEHD is complex. Genes do not have a direct effect on mental health or behaviour, but they are risk factors, so that in a very difficult environment a genetic predisposition to SMEHD is more likely to be realised.

Protective factors

However, children who are at risk of SMEHD might still flourish if they have some of the following protective factors. Indeed, children who are genetically vulnerable to SMEHD can flourish with sensitive parenting. Things that help a child have a positive outcome are:

- having a wide and supportive network of friends and family;
- having good housing;
- having access to support services including pre-school education.

If a child has at least one good relationship with an adult who provides warmth and clear boundaries, who is sensitive to their needs and who supports their education, that considerably increases their chances of doing well.

Also, if the adults caring for a child who is at risk of SMEHD are 'mind minded', this can also contribute to positive outcomes. Being 'mind minded' means they talk to the child about how they and others are thinking and feeling.

Good communication skills are also a protective factor, which is why it is vital to help a child develop these skills as early as possible.

It should be noted that having English as an additional language is not a risk factor for SMEHD, although it may impair access to information and services.

Diagnoses

SMEHD in the early years can be an indication of particular developmental disorders or mental health diagnoses. It is difficult to make a diagnosis before the age of five, but sometimes this is possible. Diagnosis can be complicated, because it is common for children to have more than one mental health or developmental problem, and they can be difficult to tell apart. Also, behaviours can be due to a variety of causes. For example, a child might not do as they are asked because they did not understand the instruction, because they have Conduct Disorder, or because they do not realise a request requires a response.

Those who know a child best, usually their parents, are often able to spot changes of behaviour or distress which could be significant. However, even those who are not involved in the diagnostic process need to try to understand each child as an individual and appreciate all of their strengths and needs in order to support their development.

Attention Deficit Hyperactivity Disorder

All toddlers are restless, inattentive and distractible, but some children have a much more significant difficulty in these three areas than their peers. Attention Deficit Hyperactivity Disorder (ADHD) can be diagnosed when a child is three or older, and usually it is obvious before the age of seven. ADHD is diagnosed if a child's development is affected by serious inattention, hyperactivity and impulsivity in all situations.

Children with ADHD might have other problems such as not being very co-operative, but this is not part of ADHD. Children with ADHD frequently also have SLCN; their language may be slow to develop and then they might have all sorts of difficulties understanding language, organising what they say and communicating appropriately with others.

Younger children can have problems controlling the volume of their voices and finding it hard not to interrupt others. They may find it difficult to listen, especially in a noisy or distracting environment, so they often hear just part of what is said.

Some children with ADHD have relatively good language skills, but still have problems with the ability to hold and manipulate information which affects their ability to learn language, read and do maths.

Autism Spectrum Disorder

An Autism Spectrum Disorder (ASD) can be diagnosed if a child has problems with social interaction and social communication as well as restricted interests and rigid and repetitive behaviours (see Chapter 8). Although a child might show these sorts of problems from a very young age, ASD is not always diagnosed early. Clearly communication difficulties are a key part of this diagnosis. In pre-school children, language development might be delayed or there might even be regression where children appear to lose language they once had. These children might use non-speech sounds to communicate, for example, barking like a dog, or they may have an unusual, perhaps monotonous intonation.

Children with ASD sometimes overuse favourite words or phrases and prefer to use single words, even if they have the ability to use sentences. They might not respond when spoken to, although they can hear and understand, and they are typically uninterested in interacting with others. If they do interact they often do so in an odd or inappropriate way. Older children, from five years of age, might have difficulty with a two-way conversation and often misunderstand sarcasm, idiom and metaphor. They can find it difficult to adapt their language to the situation and might not be aware of socially accepted behaviour.

Conduct Disorder

Children who show a consistent pattern of negative, hostile or defiant behaviour, for example, frequent and severe tantrums, might be diagnosed with Conduct Disorder. These children are also likely to have problems with social communication and using language to manage and talk about emotions.

Phobias

Some children experience serious anxiety or phobias, including anxieties about separation or being with people. Selective mutism, where children only feel able to talk in some situations, is seen by some as a social phobia, and although these children also tend to be anxious, this is probably as a consequence of this phobia (Johnson and Wintgens 2001).

Effects of abuse/neglect

Those who have been abused or neglected are very likely to experience Reactive Attachment Disorder and/or Post-Traumatic Stress Disorder as well other SMEHD. Children who have had severely disrupted early relationships often have serious problems developing relationships as they grow up. They might be emotionally unresponsive, withdrawn, aggressive or fearful.

Neglect is traumatic for a child and it has a major impact on their development. They may show aggression, regression in skills such as speech and toileting, as well as anxiety and fears.

We also know that children with attachment difficulties have poorer language skills than others, and that abuse and neglect can have serious effects on a child's development including their ability to develop communication skills.

Links between SLCN and SMEHD

Children with various SMEHD also have speech, language and communication needs, and in children with ADHD it commonly co-occurs.

It is also the case that children who have SLCN are at increased risk of developing a variety of SMEHD, especially if they have problems understanding language. Not being able to communicate can lead to anxiety, frustration, sometimes anger and often isolation. However, we must remember that every child is different and many children with SLCN and SMEHD progress well. Where young people with communication needs have a supportive family and friends their wellbeing as young adults is no different from other young people.

Social Communication Disorder

Social (Pragmatic) Communication Disorder is very common in children who have SMEHD. With this disorder children have problems using language to interact – for example:

- greeting appropriately;
- being able to change what they say depending on the listener and the setting/context;
- taking turns in a conversation;
- using the context to help understand what people are saying.

These sorts of difficulties are likely to occur in children who have SMEHD, particularly those with Conduct Disorder, Reactive Attachment Disorder and ADHD.

Most importantly, many children with SMEHD also have SLCN which might not be recognised. Research has shown that about half of all children with SMEHD also have undetected SLCN. We should be alert to the possibility of SLCN whenever a child seems to have a SMEHD, because the two frequently occur together. If it is overlooked this can mean a child is misunderstood and does not receive the support they need, putting them at risk of long-term negative consequences.

Why do speech, language and communication needs in SMEHD matter?

If a child's communication needs are not recognised they are at risk of being misunderstood.

- If a child does not follow instructions, it might be because they do not understand them or they might not know how to say they have not understood.
- If they agree to something it may be because they are trying to please without really understanding.
- If they do not explain why they have done something, it may be because they do not have the necessary vocabulary or they may not be able to construct sentences or form explanations in a clear way.

- If a child has difficulty playing with others, they might not know what to say or how to join in successfully.
- If they have lots of fights and disagreements, it may be because they do not have the language skills to problem-solve or negotiate.

Whenever a child's behaviour is a concern we need to consider their communication skills as well as how adults are communicating with them. Are we assuming they have language and social communication skills that they have not developed yet? If we simplify what we say and teach the communication skills they lack, do they behave in a more acceptable way?

Links between language and behaviour

Being aware of a child's SLCN is necessary before planning a behavioural intervention. Children who cannot understand language well often do not realise it themselves, and even if they do they may not be able to explain the problem. Many children do not really understand terms like 'consequences', or words for thoughts and feelings which we frequently use when talking about behaviour.

We tend to use complex language to think about consequences, weigh up options or think about other people's points of view. For example, 'How would you feel if he did that to you?' is a linguistically complicated question, beyond the grasp of many children with SLCN. Sometimes a child's negative response to such questions can lead to further miscommunication and misinterpretation of the child's behaviour. Therefore, considering possible SLCN in children is also very important if we are going to be successful in explaining how we want them to behave, and why.

Friendships/relationships

Children who have difficulty with social communication skills have problems working with and playing with other children. This has an impact on their education, but more crucially on the development of friendships. Being able to build good relationships and having friends are key aspects of social support, quality of life and mental health. Also we learn language and social communication skills through interacting with others, so those children who are left out miss learning opportunities and can become even more isolated without intervention. Some children are inaccurately seen as 'naughty' rather than as lacking vital social communication skills.

Expressing emotions

The development of language and emotional skills are intertwined. Some children find communicating itself stressful because it does not come easily.

For others their limited language skills add to problems with managing their emotions. We use words to talk and think about emotions and how we should behave, but some children have very limited 'emotion' vocabularies. Using words to think, or 'inner speech', is often how we calm ourselves and think things through, which can be problematic for children with SLCN.

Others with SLCN have particular difficulty learning language, especially grammar and abstract concepts like emotions and thoughts. We also know that being able to tell a story about what happened to us or what we did, in a coherent way, is important for mental health, but children with SLCN might not have the linguistic tools to do this.

Links to literacy

Another reason why SLCN matters is that children who have early difficulties with language are at risk of having literacy difficulties. If a child does not understand very well what people say, they will have difficulty understanding what they read. If they find it hard to work out how words are made up of sounds, they will find it hard to read. If they find it problematic to put sentences together when they speak, they will have similar difficulties with writing.

Overall, problems with understanding or using spoken language have a huge negative impact on learning in school, not least because most teaching is delivered in spoken language. If children cannot learn through reading, and perhaps find it difficult to concentrate, they are at risk of getting into trouble and this can be the beginning of a 'slippery slope' into disaffection.

We know that good speech and language skills act as a protective factor which reduces the likelihood of problems at school and later SMEHD. The reverse is also true; SLCN is a risk factor for more negative outcomes in terms of education, SMEHD, employment and offending behaviour (Snow and Powell 2012). We need to be aware of the communication difficulties a child faces so that we can support them in the most effective way.

How can we help?

Work collaboratively

Various professionals might be involved in the assessment and intervention with a child with SMEHD, for example education staff, school nurses, school counsellors or educational psychologists and speech and language therapists. Perhaps a GP or health visitor might be involved, as well as some of the variety of professionals who often work together in Child and Adolescent Mental Health Services (CAMHS), such as psychologists, psychiatrists and psychotherapists. Communication among the professionals working with a child and family, as well as with the family themselves, is vital, so we can all do our part to make sure the child's needs are identified and that they have the right support.

Teach the skills

The first and most effective thing we can do is to try to understand what skills a child with SLCN and SMEHD lacks and teach them. Just addressing the problematic behaviour can be ineffective because a child is often unable to behave as expected due to a 'skills gap'. As we have seen, SLCN often produce an unrecognised skills gap in children with SMEHD.

Understand the behaviour

Another reason why concentrating on behaviour is not always useful is that the same behaviours could occur in different children for different reasons and would therefore be helped by different approaches. Children might be inattentive because they are anxious, bored, or have ADHD. It may be that they do not understand what is being said, either because English is an additional language for them or because they have SLCN; or it may be because they are being asked to do something beyond their capability. Therefore, understanding the cause is important.

We need to look closely at their behaviour to try to understand when it happens, where and under what circumstances. So, if a child tends to get under the table whenever a new activity begins, it may be that they are anxious because they do not understand the verbal explanation. If there is lots of conflict during play, it may be because the child is not able to ask for a turn in an acceptable way.

Speech and language therapy assessment

Observations in context are very useful, but sometimes a speech and language therapy assessment is necessary to identify areas of communicative strength and need.

Different approaches to intervention

In order to collaborate successfully it is helpful to understand the perspectives and contributions of different professionals. The following approaches can help us understand and support children with SMEHD.

- *Humanistic* The focus here is on the quality of the relationship, including how we build children's self-esteem by showing that we value them, even if we don't like their behaviour.

- *Behavioural* This is about rewarding positive behaviour in order to encourage it. A consistent response is what makes this effective, so clear boundaries regarding behaviour are important.
- *Cognitive* This is how we teach children to think about how their behaviour has consequences. It also includes learning about ways to make themselves calm down or make themselves feel better.
- *Psychodynamic* This helps us understand how children who have had disrupted early interactions often continue to have problems forming relationships.
- *Ecological* This approach includes thinking about how the environment affects behaviour. Some children may need quiet; others need lots of space in which to be active.
- *Systemic* This approach emphasises that children belong to families, are involved in nursery or school and are part of a particular culture. To support children effectively we have to get to know and work with whatever 'systems' they belong to, particularly the family system.
- *Social learning* Children learn from those around them, so it is useful for them to have good role models in the form of other children and adults.
- *Neuroscience* This is increasingly helping us understand how children's brains develop and what we can do to help children who have experienced great stress in their early years. To learn more about any of these approaches see the Young Minds website.

We need to try to work out what a child is communicating through unacceptable behaviour, and in order to teach them communicative alternatives we can draw on all of these approaches to develop language and communication skills. Speech and language therapists can contribute to this by helping adults create the right communication environment and optimal interactions. They can also suggest evidence-based ways to help language develop.

Support the family

Looking after a child who has SMEHD and SLCN often puts great strain on a family and limits their energy to problem-solve, so offering empathy and non-judgemental support is helpful. Good support should be flexible to the needs of the child and family. Working in collaboration with the family is also crucial for success, since they know the child best, so throughout any work professionals undertake with children, their parents need to be involved and their contribution valued. Charities such as the Communication Trust and factsheets from the Royal College of Psychiatrists (*Mental Health and Growing Up: factsheets for parents, teachers and young people*) can also be helpful sources of information and support for families.

Develop positive, responsive relationships with children

As soon as a baby is born he or she is keen to interact. If adults are able to be sensitive to what a baby or child is trying to communicate, and they respond accordingly, this encourages further interaction. It is through these early, and hopefully continuing, positive interactions that babies and children develop their language, communication, thinking and emotional skills. So the best place to start if a child has difficulty with communicating and learning language is to try to develop a positive responsive relationship with them. This involves the following behaviours.

- Being attentive to the child and showing we're interested and curious.
- Waiting and listening carefully.
- Showing that we've heard and understood, by nodding and smiling.
- Talking about what the child is interested in, including feelings, and generally following their lead.
- Taking equal turns with them in conversation and play, pausing to leave a space for them to join in. Talking to a child is much less useful for their language development than engaging them in conversation; they need opportunities to listen and talk.
- Smiling, being friendly and playful as appropriate.
- Commenting on what they are doing – for example, 'I like that colour'.
- Carefully questioning. Using testing questions such as, 'What do you know about that?' can stop the conversation. Trying to minimise them and using genuine questions instead such as 'Wow, what's that?' would be more beneficial.
- Being empathic; accepting their perspective even if you don't agree.
- Judging the right amount of support and providing it, so they can be successful and learn to do things for themselves.

Parenting programmes

Emotionally responsive interactions like those described above help to shape the developing brain. Even if a child has had a very difficult start, such interactions can help a child develop the emotional and language skills they need. Sometimes it is difficult to become attuned to a child in this way because they might have difficulty interacting; for example, if the child has ASD or ADHD. Various parenting programmes can help in this respect, such as the Incredible Years (Webster-Stratton 2009). Also Video Interaction Guidance (Kennedy et al. 2009) can help if adults find it hard to get 'in tune' with a child. It can help find the successful moments in an interaction which can then be built on and developed further.

Be an emotional coach

Parents who are 'mind-minded' and talk about how they and other people think and feel have children who are more cooperative, empathic and who are better at understanding things from someone else's point of view. This understanding of someone else's perspective is very important for behaving well. It helps us recognise why people behave the way they do and to consider how our actions might affect others' thoughts and feelings. Children who have SMEHD often have problems understanding emotions, so they can benefit from this kind of 'emotional coaching', which can be provided by any adult, or even by other children.

Emotional coaching is where someone:

- Explains emotions as they happen, especially complex ones.
- Helps children notice key emotional cues in themselves, in others and in stories. These might be verbal or non-verbal and can be hard for children to identify.
- Encourages children to talk about feelings, giving them opportunities to do so, but not trying to force the issue.
- Helps a child learn to calm down by suggesting a variety of options. Movement can be very effective; relaxing by being still and trying to breathe more slowly, or getting up and moving around.
- Uses and explains words like 'think', 'know', 'believe', 'remember'.

Developing children's vocabulary to describe emotions

Children who have SLCN may find learning vocabulary particularly difficult, especially abstract emotion words, so they will need more repetition and clearer explanations than other children. If children have difficulty learning new words we may need to choose a small number to focus on, perhaps words such as 'happy, sad, scared, disgusted, surprised and angry' to start with. Then there needs to be an agreement about how these will be explained, as a variety of definitions can confuse, although a variety of examples are useful. It can also help a child to remember a new word, to talk about what sort of word it is (a feelings word), what sound it starts with and to look at pictures of faces which illustrate the emotion.

It is often effective to use a problematic situation as an opportunity to learn rather than just trying to stop the behaviour. This is sometimes known as 'name it to tame it' (Siegal and Payne Bryson 2011), so an adult can help a child understand what happened by encouraging discussion, although it is usually necessary to have some time to calm down before doing this. The adult can offer labels for the feelings the child experienced, although we should not assume we know how someone else is feeling but simply offer suggestions. Such discussion can also help a child understand the order of events, as well as other people's feelings. We know that just naming an emotion can help us to calm down.

Help children develop their social communication skills

Within a positive responsive relationship adults can help a child develop their language and communication skills by using the following strategies.

- Modelling the language they need. So if they are getting angry because another child wants a toy they are playing with, we could suggest they say 'You can have it next', or 'This is really hard for me, it's my favourite', or 'I'm getting very cross, I need to go and run.'
- Suggesting what they could do, so if we think they haven't understood something, say 'Maybe you need to ask a question?'
- Giving specific praise for good communication skills, e.g. 'Great, you asked for a turn.'
- Making sure they understand what is likely to happen in situations they find tricky, perhaps during free play or at lunch times.

Developing children's play skills

As we know, children with SMEHD often have difficulty with social communication. They have difficulty using language with others effectively and they may need to be taught these skills. If we want to encourage a child to play with others, although this is something they repeatedly fail at, we need to earn their trust by developing a positive responsive relationship with them as described above. If we give them our attention and follow their lead, then they might follow ours. Being non-judgemental about what they do in play (as long as they and others are safe) and encouraging creative imaginative play will hopefully help them develop their enjoyment and engagement in play. They will also benefit from our being an appreciative audience for anything they create.

We might also need to set up activities for children who struggle to interact, so they can enjoy playing with each other. It is helpful if we can include children who have good social communication skills to provide role models, but also younger ones with whom to practise such skills. Adults can set up all sorts of interactive games for children; these can include playground-type games such as chase or hide and seek, as well as opportunities to practise turn-taking in simple board games. We can also encourage children to take on particular roles, as in LEGO therapy (LeGoff et al. 2014) where one child decides what to build, another finds the pieces, and a third is the builder. With appropriate support from adults children can practise many language skills in this sort of game, such as describing, explaining, checking they have understood what someone else has said, and checking that someone has understood their instructions.

Role play

Children may also need support and encouragement to take part in the sort of role play activities that most children enjoy. The language skills required to negotiate who will be Batman, or who gets to be a dog, are sophisticated and might need to be modelled. The adults supporting may also have to model and suggest ideas for play itself; in the 'shop', 'garage' or 'restaurant'. It is helpful to follow the child's lead here too as creative play can reduce anxiety, but obviously if a child is not skilled at interacting, playing with someone else can be a very stressful experience. It is crucial to have fun while playing. However, if things do go wrong it offers further opportunities for emotional coaching, perhaps by talking about frustration and how to deal with it.

Speech and language therapists and others may also use techniques such as video feedforward where editing is used to show a child a video of themselves succeeding at something they currently find difficult, such as greeting people appropriately. Social stories may also be used to help children develop their social communication skills, in addition to supporting children as they interact naturally.

Encourage story telling

We know that being able to 'tell the story' of something difficult that happened to us helps us feel better about it and enables us to 'move on' from it. These narrative skills are also important for literacy and for learning in general. However, children with SLCN often have problems with storytelling because it requires high level language skills, so we might have to support children in learning to tell and understand stories.

Setting up the structure

It can help children to learn about the structure of stories if adults ask and answer questions like: 'Who's in it? Where are they? What happened? Why? How did he feel? What happened in the end?' Children with SLCN can find these questions hard to understand so they may need to focus on one at a time.

Cause and effect

Stories are also useful to help children understand cause and effect as well as the words that describe it, such as 'so' and 'because'. Stories enable children to understand the effects events can have on characters' thoughts and feelings, although it is useful to have some sort of visual support, a picture book or prompt pictures for the key points. Stories are not just those in books, but also ones the children make up, act out with toys or listen to. Not every child can sit on a mat and listen to a whole story, but all can have fun with a story that is simple enough for them to understand, and that is related to their interests. Speech and language therapists might work specifically on grammar and narrative skills but everyone can engage children in storytelling.

Stories as aids to solving problems

Children might need help in working out how real problems or disagreements and consequences relate to each other. There is often a lot to remember and it may be difficult for the children to get the sequence of events in the right order. So, as well as practising telling the story, it can be helpful to write it down (adults can be the child's scribe) or draw it out, perhaps in cartoon form. Acting it out or acting through toys can also help a complex situation make sense when a child has trouble understanding words or telling a story in a clear and coherent way. If it is emotionally difficult to think about inappropriate behaviour, suggest they 'fast forward and rewind' in their mind, so they can focus on the problem solving rather than the unpleasant parts. Siegal and Payne Bryson (2011) suggest that it is possible for some children to focus in this way from six years onwards.

Raise children's self esteem

Self-esteem is important because it is an indicator of good mental health, and once children develop their confidence they will be able to make the most of opportunities to learn. They can develop their confidence and self-esteem when adults are responsive to their needs.

Problem-solving

One way of developing self-confidence is by encouraging problem-solving in children, offering support where they need it but enabling them to do as much as they can by themselves. Children may need reassurance to try new things and it might be necessary to teach problem-solving skills specifically by:

- encouraging them to talk about what they want to achieve;
- discussing what is and what is not working as they try to problem-solve;
- asking them to think about alternative ways to solve the problem and how useful each of these possibilities might be.

This would provide another opportunity to talk about feelings and how they affect our ability to problem-solve. Once the children have succeeded they can be encouraged to talk about what worked and why.

Throughout this process adults can offer suggestions for vocabulary, ways to describe and explain, and ways to solve the problem. They might say things such as, 'Sometimes if that happens I try this...' The adults can acknowledge the feelings that arise as well as providing ideas about how to manage those feelings. For example, they might say, 'Is it annoying? Shall we take a break?' They can also encourage children to ask each other for help.

Use of praise

Praise is useful to raise self-esteem, but only if it is genuine and specific – for example, 'I liked the way you checked he was listening before you explained.' Adults need to be alert so they can notice and comment on positive behaviour rather than focussing on 'difficult' behaviours. It is helpful to encourage children to use this sort of praise to talk about what they have achieved, and to praise each other. It also helps to praise for effort, because sometimes they will try and not succeed, but they still need to be encouraged.

Adults can model positive ways to think about failure, for example by saying 'Oh well. Never mind. I can try again', rather than saying 'I am rubbish and no good at anything.' Non-verbal praise such as a smile is often very powerful too, as is asking children to reflect on difficulties they have already overcome and how they did that.

It is clearly not useful to ridicule or try to shame a child; this can lead to a further lowering of self-esteem and increase SMEHD. Saying 'No!' releases stress hormones in the recipient (Siegal and Payne Bryson 2011) and can reduce their ability to think. Although it may be necessary to make it clear that we do not like a child's behaviour, we also need to offer an encouraging alternative. Saying 'Yes, I understand why you did that but I'd rather you asked first' is more likely to produce hormones that can help the child feel better about themselves and learn to behave in a more acceptable way.

Developing our own emotional and communication skills

All adults interacting with children with SMEHD and SLCN will sometimes have to deal with difficult behaviour. This provides an opportunity to practise our own emotion-management skills, and to model ways to manage emotions positively.

An important part of helping a child to calm down if they are very upset and angry is staying calm ourselves and trying to reduce the volume and complexity of our language. Another key way to defuse a difficult situation and to help manage our own emotions is to focus on listening to the child's point of view and trying to understand it fully before adding our thoughts. When anyone is upset they can't think clearly and need to calm down first, so trying to reason with an angry child often makes matters worse. The following might be useful to calm a stressful situation.

- Listen carefully to their view and empathise with their feelings even if you don't agree.
- Use a calm, confident tone of voice.
- Make sure your expectations are easy to understand.
- Use positive language, tone of voice and non-verbal communication.
- Tactically ignore some of the behaviours as this can be effective.
- Distract them.
- Assume a playful intent, or give them the benefit of the doubt.
- Use positive humour.

When things are calmer:

- Be willing to negotiate, show trust and respect.
- Explain the effect of their behaviour on others' emotions, including your own.

Again, difficult situations are opportunities to learn for everyone involved. Children can learn negotiation skills when these are modelled by adults, especially if they are encouraged to take an active role. For example, you might say 'Can you think of a way to solve this that would make everyone happy?'

Conclusion

Every child with signs of social emotional or mental health difficulties should be screened for SLCN. We need to identify problems in language and communication development early and also remain alert to the possibility of SLCN as children's language development can become compromised at any stage. Adults need to provide plenty of language learning opportunities and should interact with children in ways which will help their language and communication skills develop. There are many different ways to help children develop the language and communication skills they need to interact well. If we implement these early enough it will hopefully mean that children are less likely to have continuing difficulties in interacting, learning and indeed with social, emotional and mental health.

References

Johnson, M. and Wintgens, A. (2001) *The Selective Mutism Resource Manual.* Milton Keynes: Speechmark.

Kennedy, H., Landor, M. and Todd, L. (Eds.) (2011) *Video Interaction Guidance: A relationship-based intervention to promote attunement, empathy and wellbeing.* London: Jessica Kingsley Publishers.

Law, J., McBean, K. and Rush, R. (2011) Communication skills in a population of primary school-aged children raised in an area of pronounced social disadvantage. *International Journal of Language and Communication Disorders, 46, 657–664.*

LeGoff, D.B., Gomez De La Cuesta, G., Krauss, G.W. and Baron-Cohen, S. (2014) *LEGO®-Based Therapy: How to build social competence through LEGO®-based clubs for children with autism and related conditions.* London: Jessica Kingsley Publishers.

Royal College of Psychiatrists (4th edition) *Mental Health and Growing Up: Factsheets for parents, teachers and young people.* www.rcpsych.ac.uk/publications/books/rcpp/

Siegal, D. and Payne Bryson, T. (2011) *The Whole Brain Child.* London: Constable and Robinson Ltd.

Snow, P. and Powell, M. (2012) Youth (in)justice: Oral language competence in early life and risk for engagement in antisocial behaviour in adolescence [online]. *Trends and Issues in Crime and Criminal Justice, 435,* [1]–[6].

Webster-Stratton, C. (2009) *The Incredible Years: A trouble shooting guide for parents of children aged 2–8 years.* Seattle: The Incredible Years.

Young Minds www.youngminds.org.uk/

Further reading

The Communication Trust www.thecommunicationtrust.org.uk

The Council for Awards in Care, Health and Education Level 3 Diploma for Children's Care, Learning and Development (Wales and Northern Ireland) (QCF) has an optional unit (CYpop22) entitled Understand the speech, language and communication needs of children and young people with behavioural, social and emotional difficulties www.cache.org.uk/Qualifications/CYP/CYPL3/Documents/

Cross, M. (2011) (2nd edition) *Children with social emotional and behavioural difficulties and communication problems: There is always a reason.* London: Jessica Kingsley Publishers.

Chapter 8

Autism spectrum disorder

Tom Loucas

What is Autism Spectrum Disorder?

Autism Spectrum Disorder (ASD) is a common difficulty found in young children. It affects over one in one hundred children in the UK (Baird et al. 2006). All children are different and it is the same with children with ASD. No two children with ASD will behave in the same way. However, children with ASD do share some general features of behaviour. These include:

1 difficulties with language used for communication;
2 difficulties with social interaction;
3 restricted or intense interests and repetitive behaviours.

(WHO 1993)

The spectrum

The range of behaviours shown in children with ASD and the degree to which each child is affected will vary, so that the difficulties seen in children with autism are described as being on 'a spectrum'. ASD is more common in boys than girls and is often associated with other developmental difficulties such as learning disabilities and mental health difficulties.

Causes and risk factors

The exact causes of ASD are not yet clear, but there is strong evidence to suggest a genetic cause. ASD runs in families and if one child is affected there is an increased likelihood of another child in the same family having ASD. The precise genes involved in increased risk of ASD have yet to be identified, but it is clear that many different genes are involved. The National Institute for Health and Clinical Excellence (NICE 2011) identifies other factors that increase the risk of having an autistic spectrum disorder. If a child has another chromosomal condition, such as Down's syndrome, or a genetic condition such as Fragile X syndrome, they will be at greater risk of having an autistic spectrum disorder. In the same way, a child with birth defects associated with problems with brain development, such as cerebral palsy, children with general developmental delays, and those with epilepsy will also be at risk.

How is Autism Spectrum Disorder recognised and diagnosed?

There is no medical test that will identify ASD, so the diagnosis is made on the basis of talking to parents about their child's development and observing how the child interacts, communicates and plays. Before a child can be referred for a diagnostic assessment the risk of a possible ASD needs to be identified.

NICE Guidelines

NICE has developed a specific guideline for recognition, referral and diagnosis of children with ASD based on the best available evidence (NICE 2011). This guideline includes advice about features of development that should alert professionals working with young children and their parents to the possibility of ASD in a particular child about whom concerns have been raised.

The NICE guideline lists a number of signs and symptoms of possible ASD that might be manifest in a child or young person. In the following section the three general features of behaviour listed above will be considered in detail in relation to a young child with ASD.

Difficulties with language used for communication

Problems with language and communication may be seen as a delay in spoken language. For example, a child of two years of age may be saying fewer than ten words. Sometimes a child may use language for communication infrequently – for example, using only single words despite being able to speak in sentences. In some cases a child may lose the use of language after it has been acquired.

Loss of language after a child has started to talk, typically occurring in the second year of life, can be considered a 'red flag' for ASD. Parents report a loss of language in over thirty per cent of children who go on to receive an ASD diagnosis (Baird et al. 2008).

Difficulties with social interaction

Problems with social interaction may be manifest, for example when a child does not respond to their name being called, even though their hearing is known to be normal. There may be a lack or a reduced amount of smiling in social situations, particularly in response to another person. There may also be a generally reduced, or lack of, response to other people's facial expressions or feelings. A child may offer cuddles to their parent, but reject cuddles when they are offered by the parent. A child may also show unusually negative responses when asked to do something by another person – sometimes referred to as 'demand avoidant behaviour'.

Interest in others

Problems interacting with others may also include a limited awareness of personal space, or a strong reaction to other people entering their own personal space. A child may show little social interest in others, including their peers. In some children this may go as far as rejecting contact with others. If a child is interested in other children, s/he may approach them inappropriately, and may seem to be aggressive or disruptive. A child who has problems with interaction may not be able to imitate others' actions, such as the initiation of social play with others. They may show a distinct preference for playing alone. Such a child may not enjoy social situations that most children like – for example, birthday parties.

Non-verbal communication behaviours

Even when the child is enjoying an activity, it may not be apparent since s/he may not share their enjoyment through comments, facial expression and other typical behaviours.

Other difficulties with social interaction include poor use of non-verbal communication behaviours such as eye contact, pointing and general use of gestures. Although the child may place the adult's hand on an object in order to get help, they will not necessarily use gestures and facial expressions to communicate.

Joint attention

The development of joint attention is part of the development of social interaction skills in most young children. However, in young children who have difficulties with social interaction, joint attention may typically be reduced or even lacking. A child may lack the ability to look where the other person is looking, or to follow where the other person is pointing. The child may look at the person's hand instead.

Restricted or intense interests and repetitive behaviours

These may be seen as a lack of imagination and variety in pretend play. The child may have unusual or restricted interests and/or rigid and repetitive behaviours. For example, they may insist on watching the same DVD over and over again. There may be repetitive movements such as hand flapping, body rocking while standing or sitting, spinning, or finger flicking. The child's play may be repetitive or stereotyped, for example opening and closing doors. The child may have an excessive insistence on following their own agenda. They may show extreme emotional reactions to change or new situations and insist on things always being the same. Some children have an over- or under-reaction to sensations, for example textures, sounds or smells. Some children may have an extreme reaction to food, for example, an excessive reaction to the smell, taste, texture or appearance of food. They may have extreme food fads.

Signs of ASD before the age of two

Recent research has uncovered less dramatic signs of possible ASD before the age of two. Zwaigenbaum and colleagues (2009) found that between twelve and eighteen months, infants who go on to develop ASD can be distinguished from typically developing children in a number of areas.

- *Visual skills* A child at risk of ASD may have an unusual way of watching objects as they move and may show a fixation on objects.
- *Motor skills* A child may show reduced activity levels, and delayed fine and gross motor development.
- *Play skills* Children may show delayed development in copying actions, limited toy play, and repetitive actions with toys.
- *Social communication skills* With regard to social communication, differences may include unusual eye gaze, lack of looking at the person when their name is called, a lack of social smiling and copying.
- *Demonstrating emotion* The child may also show extreme emotional responses to ordinary situations and a reduced expression of positive emotion.
- *Babbling* There may be a delay in babbling, especially to-and-fro social babbling.
- *Cognitive skills* The development of thinking and learning abilities may be slower than in a typically developing child when tested by a health professional.
- *Differentiating factors between children with ASD and children with developmental delays* A number of early unusual behaviours also distinguish between infants who go on to develop ASD and those with other developmental delays, including language delay. These behaviours

include unusual exploration of toys, repetitive movements, reduced social communication, and reduced, or lack of, sharing of positive emotion.

Referral

Once concern about a possible ASD is established a child will be referred for a diagnostic assessment. The referral for an assessment will usually come from a professional who works with the child. Health and early years workers take seriously any concerns expressed by parents about a child's behaviour or development, even if they or other professionals do not share them. If a parent has a concern it is essential to discuss it with their GP, health visitor, community nurse or other health professional.

The autism team

NICE (2011) recommends that in 'best practice' assessment should be carried out by a multidisciplinary group, the autism team. This will include a paediatrician and/or child and adolescent psychiatrist, a speech and language therapist and a clinical and/or educational psychologist. Other professionals whose expertise can be called on include an occupational therapist, a specialist health visitor or nurse, a specialist teacher, or a social worker. The autism team should have specific skills and understanding in carrying out autism diagnostic assessment and communicating with children and their parents about the diagnosis.

Assessment

The assessment to diagnose an autism spectrum disorder will involve both a detailed discussion with a child's parents or carers and a direct assessment of the child. Parents will be asked about their child's development with a focus on the patterns of development and behaviours that are characteristic of children with ASD as set out in the World Health Organization's International Classification of Diseases (ICD-10; WHO 1993). This classification refers to difficulties in the areas of development affected in ASD as referred to above: communication and reciprocal social interaction, restricted interests, and repetitive behaviours.

The assessment process with the child will involve interaction and observation to consider the child's social and communication skills in order to evaluate those areas of development in terms of the diagnostic criteria set out in ICD-10. In addition to the ASD diagnostic assessment, the professionals involved in the process will need to consider other possible diagnoses and also other conditions, because, as outlined earlier, children with ASD are at a greater risk of other developmental, medical, and mental and behavioural conditions.

Diagnosis

A diagnosis, if it is offered, will be based on all of the information gathered from talking to the parents and direct assessment of the child, as described above. The diagnosis and its implications will be carefully explained and parents or carers will be provided with information about support that may be available locally.

However, parents will react differently to such a diagnosis. They may need time to process the information, particularly if English is an additional language. They may need time to consider the implications for the child and the family and to have further discussions with other family members. With hindsight they may have further questions and there may be other cultural issues to consider. Therefore, best practice is to offer parents a follow-up appointment within six weeks of the diagnostic assessment to give time for further discussion.

What works supporting children with ASD?

Many approaches to supporting children with ASD have been proposed. Although there is no 'cure', much can be done to help the children and their families. Parents will want to know which approach will work best for their child now, but which will also have the most benefits for their child's development in the long term.

Current research is not able to offer clear-cut answers for parents. However, there are ways of supporting children that are effective in developing the child's skills in the main areas of difficulty seen in ASD, and in reducing the behaviours which may interfere with their everyday life.

For example, there are some comprehensive programmes which aim to address the range of behaviours which are typically seen in ASD. Other approaches offer a narrower focus on specific aspects of development and behaviour, such as language and communication difficulties.

Evaluating intervention programmes (see also Chapter 9)

Research Autism, a UK charity, lists over a thousand interventions that have been suggested for children with ASD (2013). The range includes:

- medication;
- diet and nutritional interventions;
- behaviour and development programmes;
- education and learning programmes.

While this extensive list appears to offer parents a wide range of options to choose from, unfortunately many of these interventions lack evidence for their effectiveness. Even where there is evidence that a particular treatment works, it is important to look at the results from many studies, not just one. This is because while one study may suggest an approach is effective, another may not find positive results. Pooling the evidence from as many studies as possible provides a much better guide to the effectiveness of an intervention. In addition, because all children with ASD are different and are affected by ASD in individual ways, any programme of support will need to be tailored to the individual child's needs and those of his or her family. Parents need opportunities to discuss with the professionals who are working with them the evidence for what works, their child's needs and their own preferences for support.

NICE (2013) has produced a guideline on the management and support of children with ASD which draws on the evidence for what works. In the US the Agency for Healthcare Research and Quality (AHRQ 2011) has also completed a review of 159 studies of interventions to support children with ASD which might help parents and professionals make decisions about how to support children with ASD most effectively. The AHRQ concluded that there were some interventions that showed promise, but the evidence should be treated with caution.

Behavioural approaches

Both NICE and AHRQ reviewed many different approaches including behavioural, educational, medical and therapeutic interventions. In the following section the focus will be on behavioural and educational programmes for which there has been some evidence of effectiveness.

Behaviour programmes can be used when working with children on many areas of development, including attention, play and self-help skills, as well as language and communication. Such programmes can also be used when working with children with challenging behaviour. There are different types of behaviour programmes but they all use an approach called Applied Behaviour Analysis to teach new skills.

Applied Behaviour Analysis (ABA)

The studies reviewed by AHRQ showed positive effects of ABA on children's language, thinking and reasoning, and daily living skills.

ABA is based on the following principles:

- a behaviour that is rewarded is more likely to be repeated;
- a behaviour if not rewarded will diminish.

In ABA approaches, the behaviour to be learnt is often broken down into small steps for teaching and each step is taught one at a time.

- There is a target behaviour.
- The professionals working with the child use motivating rewards for the child.
- These rewards reinforce the target behaviour when it occurs.

In the reviews, the programmes that worked best required a well-trained ABA therapist who worked one-to-one with the child for more than thirty hours a week over a period of one to three years. In practice, the level of intensity of thirty hours a week for so many years may not be possible. For the family, the intensive nature of such a programme can make severe demands on everyday life and family routines would need to be adjusted to make room for the work on the programme.

The Picture Exchange Communication System

The Picture Exchange Communication System (PECS) is an example of one way in which the ABA approach has been applied to communication (Bondy and Frost 1994). PECS was originally developed to be used with children with Autism Spectrum Disorder in order to help them develop communication skills. It has also been used with a range of children who have communication and cognitive difficulties, as a form of augmentative and alternative communication. It needs to be used by a trained practitioner.

PECS is a highly structured behavioural approach which uses modelling (see Chapter 2) and prompting to teach the child functional communication. It teaches the child to communicate using pictures, by giving the adult a picture card in exchange for the item required.

Training is divided into six phases which must be followed in the order set out by the programme.

- *Phase 1* Requesting is learnt at phase 1, where the child is taught to exchange a picture for a desired object, initially with prompting from the adult trainer. The picture will represent a highly rewarding object which hopefully will motivate the child. The initial prompts involve the trainer physically moving the child's hand to the picture.
- *Phase 2* In phase 2 the distance between the child and the trainer is increased and prompts are reduced.
- *Phase 3* The child is taught to choose the appropriate picture from a selection in a communication book or board. A communication book consists of pictures relevant to the child's needs that are specifically selected to help the child develop some basic communication skills.
- *Phase 4* In phase 4 the child learns to combine a set phrase such as 'I want' with a picture to construct a short sentence.
- *Phase 5* In this phase the child learns to respond to questions such as 'What do you want?' with pictures and/or speech.

- *Phase 6* In this final phase the child is taught to comment by responding to questions such as 'What do you see?' and 'What is it?' with pictures and/or speech.

PECS is widely used in a variety of educational settings in the UK. The AHRQ concluded that although PECS is effective at increasing the number of words used by children for up to three months after intervention, improvements do not seem to be maintained over the longer term. Equally NICE did not find strong evidence to recommend the use of PECS, but did consider the evidence promising enough to suggest further research would be useful.

Social communication programmes

NICE recommends that specific social communication programmes should be considered as part of the package of support offered to children with ASD and their families. These programmes use play-based approaches which aim to increase the joint attention of an adult and the child, focussing on the social interaction between the two and their joint engagement. In many such programmes the therapy is delivered by parents who are trained to implement the approach. (See Chapter 9 for a discussion on programmes.) One example is the More than Words programme (Girolametto et al. 2007) developed by the Hanen Centre in Canada. This programme is used by speech and language therapists in the UK. Another example is the Pre-school Autism Communication Therapy (PACT; Green et al. 2010) which was the subject of a large research study. This programme will be considered in some detail as it shares key features with other play-based social communication programmes.

Pre-school Autism Communication Therapy (PACT)

PACT uses natural interactions between a child and his or her parents to develop social communication skills. Parents attend two-hour training sessions twice a month for six months followed by monthly booster sessions for six months. Sessions are led by a speech and language therapist. Between sessions, families are asked to complete thirty minutes of daily home practice. In the sessions parents learn to adapt the way they interact with their child to maximise opportunities for the development of social communication skills. The training is supported by video work. Parent–child play sessions are videoed and these are each followed by a feedback session. In the feedback session parents are encouraged to reflect on their interaction with their child. They are given the opportunity to identify their own skills that they use to support successful communication.

Shared attention

PACT targets the main difficulties that children with ASD have with social communication. Children with ASD tend to lack the ability to share attention with an adult when relating to an object or event in the world around them. This means they have difficulties drawing an adult's attention to something they are interested in, and also have problems responding when an adult attempts to direct their attention. If a child does not share attention with an adult, s/he cannot see that gestures and words refer to things and events in the world. It is clear that shared attention is an essential part of the foundation for developing language and communication. For this reason, PACT starts by helping parents achieve periods of shared attention with their child. Establishing shared attention can be achieved by the parent waiting and carefully watching their child's focus of attention, recognising when there is an opportunity to share attention and quickly responding to it. For example, if a child is playing and looks up, the parent can respond in a way that demonstrates they are sharing attention with the child by commenting, smiling and showing pleasure in what the child is doing.

Communication skills

Communication is about conveying our thoughts, feelings and interests to someone else. This can be done with language, or non-verbally using eye contact, facial expression and/or gesture. Communication can occur as a response to someone else. It can also be used to start an interaction or to keep an interaction going. Children with ASD usually communicate less than typically developing children. When they do communicate their speech or their non-verbal communication may not be clear, or it may appear unusual and so may be difficult to recognise. PACT helps parents to recognise when their children are communicating and to support any form of communication.

Communicative intent

The idea of communicative intent is an important aspect of communication. This emerges when a child realises that his actions and vocalisations have an effect on other people. The child will then begin to intentionally communicate with others. Children with ASD initiate communication less and show a more limited range of communicative intentions than typically developing children.

A child with ASD may cry, look at an object or even name it because they want it, but the intention of the communication is unclear because s/he does not make a clear attempt to direct the adult's attention to the object they want. PACT trains parents to facilitate intentional communication by using pauses in their interactions to encourage the child to produce a communication response. This helps the child become aware of the parent as someone who responds to communication through actions and words.

Timed responses

The timing of the parent's response to their child's attempts to communicate is crucial in developing the child's social communication responsiveness. The aim is to reduce mistimed responses and to increase well-timed responses which are adapted to the child's focus. This can include commenting on the child's topic of interest and showing interest and pleasure in their play.

Parents are encouraged to follow the child's lead in play rather than trying to direct the child. Instead of making demands on the child, parents are encouraged to offer well-timed responses such as commenting. Parents are trained to identify the child's behaviours as meaningful communication and to respond to them as though the child intends to communicate.

Use of language

Parents are also trained to think about the language they use with their child and to modify it so that it matches the child's language abilities. They are asked to use language that matches the child's focus of interest and what the child is intending to communicate. This may involve the parent assuming what the child intends, but this assumption is based on careful observation of the child's focus of attention and activity.

From these foundations PACT goes on to build on the range of communication functions the child uses to support their development as an active communicator. The programme trains parents to elaborate and expand on the child's own play as well as their communication and language. This includes taking part in conversations at whatever level of language the child achieves.

The PACT study showed the programme was effective in supporting parents to provide well-timed responses to their children. It was also effective in increasing the frequency of social initiations made by the child and the amount of parent–child shared attention. Thus, the training had clear effects on those aspects of behaviour specifically targeted by the approach. However, the degree to which the intervention had benefits beyond parent–child interaction was less certain. No improvement was seen in the child's interaction with an unfamiliar adult or in the child's functioning in school, as reported by the child's teacher. Beneficial effects of the gains made during the training may emerge from further research which focusses on the long-term effects.

Learning Experiences – an Alternative Program for Pre-schoolers and their Parents (LEAP) (Philip et al. 2011)

NICE also recommends that there should be further research into the core symptoms of ASD and into the programmes which aim to support children with ASD across all their areas of need, developmental skills and daily living skills.

Learning Experiences – an Alternative Program for Pre-schoolers and their Parents (LEAP), now being used as a model for pre-school-aged children, is one such programme that shows promise. LEAP is a comprehensive approach to supporting children with ASD. It has many components and works through everyone who knows the child. Parents and other adults in the family are trained in behavioural teaching strategies. Pre-school staff are taught about what ASD is and about the LEAP programme. They are taught effective communication and teaching strategies for children with ASD and how to organise and manage a classroom so that the environment supports a child with ASD. They are also taught how to manage behaviour positively and how to support interactions with other children. Other children in the school can be trained to use LEAP. If they are given social skills training they can help to support the communication and social interaction of children with ASD.

How parents can be supported to support children with ASD

Because ASD can affect many aspects of a child's development parents can best support a child with ASD if they have a clear understanding of the condition. NICE (2013) recommends that families are given information about ASD, how it can be managed, and what support is available. Parents should expect there to be a case manager or key worker who has an overview of the child, the family and their needs, so that as these needs change appropriate support can be offered. Parents should be provided with contact details for local and national organisations that can offer support.

National organisations/programmes

The National Autistic Society (NAS)

In the UK the National Autistic Society is an excellent source of information, advice and support for parents and families as well as for individuals with ASD.

NAS EarlyBird Programme

For parents whose child has just received a diagnosis, the NAS runs parent training programmes called EarlyBird (www.autism.org.uk/earlybird) which are available in many areas of the UK. EarlyBird is delivered to a small group of families and lasts for three months. It combines group training sessions with individual home visits. Video feedback is used during the home visits to help the parents apply what they have learnt and to continue to work with their child at home.

EARLYBIRD SUPPORT

The aim of EarlyBird is to support parents to facilitate their child's social communication and appropriate behaviour in everyday settings. By offering support as early as possible the programme also helps parents to handle their child in the most effective way when he or she is still young. This can pre-empt the development of inappropriate behaviours. A key part of the programme is to provide parents with information which will enable them to better understand their child's ASD. This knowledge can help parents see the world through their child's eyes and develop more effective ways of interacting and communicating. The programme gives parents insight into problem behaviours by helping them understand why their child's ASD can lead to such behaviours.

VISUAL SUPPORT

It also explains how providing an appropriate structure can reduce the triggers for the behaviours. For instance, visual support can be effective for children who are visual learners. The National Autistic Society (2013) offers advice on ways to present information visually so that parents can support their child with different aspects of everyday living. For example, some children with ASD benefit from structure and routine which can make everyday life more predictable. One way of helping a child understand daily routines is to create a visual timetable which uses pictures or symbols to represent each activity or event in a schedule, enabling the child to more easily understand the structure of their day.

LOCAL GROUPS

The NAS has local groups run by volunteers where parents can meet other families with children with ASD. Drawing on the expertise of others is an important way for parents to find the support they need. Sharing experiences with other parents in a similar situation provides invaluable support. It may help to provide opportunities for offering advice on managing particular behaviours, knowing where to get help and how to access services.

Summary

In this chapter ASD has been discussed as a common developmental difficulty which affects how children communicate, play, interact socially and react to everyday situations. These characteristic patterns of development and behaviour help identify children who are at risk of ASD, and are used by health professionals to decide whether an ASD diagnosis is appropriate. ASD differs between children in the degree and range to which ASD behaviours are seen. Nevertheless, for any child ASD is likely to have a significant impact on everyday life for them and their family.

It is important when deciding what support to put in place for a child that parents are aware of the evidence from research studies about what works. They will benefit from having the opportunity to discuss with the professionals supporting them which programme or approach is most appropriate for them and their child.

In this chapter a number of specific behavioural and educational approaches that may be effective for children with ASD have been presented. These approaches often involve parents delivering the programme, with training and support from professionals. In addition to specific approaches, parents need information and advice about ASD. This will help them to understand their child better so they can respond in a positive way to any challenging behaviour. They will also learn how to modify the environment and everyday routines in order to minimise the chances of such behaviours occurring.

While ASD is a lifelong condition, well-supported parents can maximise the opportunities for their child's development and well-being.

References

Agency for Healthcare Research and Quality (2011) *Therapies for Children with Autism Spectrum Disorders. Comparative Effectiveness Review Number 26.* Rockville, MD: Agency for Healthcare Research and Quality.

Baird, G., Charman, T., Pickles, A., Chandler, S., Loucas, T., Meldrum, D., Carcani Rathwell, I. et al. (2008) Regression, developmental trajectory and associated problems in disorders in the autism spectrum: The SNAP study. *Journal of Autism and Developmental Disorders*, 38 (10), 1827–1836.

Baird, G., Simonoff, E., Pickles, A., Chandler, S., Loucas, T., Meldrum, D. and Charman, T. (2006) Prevalence of disorders of the autism spectrum in a population cohort of children in South Thames – the Special Needs and Autism Project (SNAP). *Lancet*, 368, 210–15.

Bondy, A.S. and Frost, L.A. (1994) The Picture Exchange Communication System. *Focus on Autism and Other Developmental Disabilities*, 9 (3), 1–19.

Girolametto, L., Sussman, S. and Weitzman, E. (2007) Using case study methods to investigate the effects of interactive intervention for children with autism spectrum disorders. *Journal of Communication Disorders*, 40 (6), 470–492.

Green, J., Charman, T., McConachie, H., Aldred, C., Slonims, V., Howlin, P., Le Couteur, A. et al. (2010) Parent-mediated communication-focused treatment in children with autism (PACT): A randomised controlled trial. *Lancet*, 375 (9732), 2152–2160.

National Institute for Health and Clinical Excellence (2011) *Autism: Recognition, referral and diagnosis of children and young people on the autism spectrum.* National Clinical Guideline Number 128. London: National Institute for Health and Clinical Excellence.

National Institute for Health and Clinical Excellence (2013) *Autism: The management and support of children and young people on the autism spectrum.* National Clinical Guideline Number 170. London: National Institute for Health and Clinical Excellence.

National Autistic Society (2013)Visual supports www.autism.org.uk/visualsupports

Phillip, S., Strain, P.S. and Bovey II, E.H. (2011) Randomized, controlled trial of the LEAP model of early intervention for young children with autism spectrum disorders. *Topics in Early Childhood Special Education*, 31, 133–154.

Research Autism (2013) *Interventions, Treatments and Therapies for Autism.* www.researchautism.net/pages/autism_treatments_therapies_interventions/2013

World Health Organization (1993) *Mental disorders: a glossary and guide to their classification in accordance with the 10th revision of the international classification of diseases – research diagnostic criteria (ICD-10).* Geneva: WHO.

Zwaigenbaum, L., Bryson, S., Lord, C., Rogers, S., Carter, A., Carver, L., Chawarska, K. et al. (2009) Clinical assessment and management of toddlers with suspected autism spectrum disorder: Insights from studies of high-risk infants. *Pediatrics*, 123 (5), 1383–1391.

Further reading

Dickinson, P. and Hannah, L. (1998) (Revised 2014) *It Can Get Better: Dealing with common behaviour problems in young children with autism.* London: The National Autistic Society.

Griffin, S. and Sandler, D. (2010) *Motivate to communicate! 300 games and activities for your child with autism.* London: Jessica Kingsley.

Wing, L. (2002) *The Autistic Spectrum: A guide for parents and professionals.* London: Constable and Robinson.

Chapter 9

Language programmes

Blanca Schaefer and Silke Fricke

Introduction

Spoken and written language build the foundation for human communication. Only by using spoken or written language can we say precisely what we think, believe or feel. Language helps us understand someone's thoughts, share what we know and express what we want to do. However, not all children develop language as expected; some may struggle to learn new words or to use certain sounds. Others may have difficulties putting words together, for example, or summarising a story.

Hence, we need to support children who struggle to develop their language skills. We need to help them to communicate effectively with their environment and successfully access the curriculum at school. This will then form the basis for active participation in society, as well as the acquisition of knowledge. Since spoken language is complex and includes a variety of skills, intervention programmes to help support such children might target one or more language areas.

This chapter begins with a summary of what interventions and programmes are and what aspects should be considered when selecting a programme. Subsequently an overview is provided about language programmes which are currently available in the UK.

Also discussed are:

- the links between spoken and written language;
- language programmes for children with English as an additional language;
- parent-based language intervention programmes;
- language intervention programmes for children with Autism Spectrum Disorder.

The chapter concludes with a comment on advances in technology in relation to language programmes.

What is language intervention?

The characteristics of different interventions vary widely. Language intervention generally means that activities and techniques are chosen in order to improve children's language and communication skills. This may include working with the children themselves using direct activities. These are often provided by specially trained or skilled people such as early years workers, teachers, teaching assistants, parents, speech and language therapists or speech and language therapy assistants.

However, intervention may also mean using indirect actions which might improve the children's communicative environment, for example. This could include working with parents to train them in using certain communicative strategies to support their child's language development. Indirect actions might also involve making changes within the setting in which the child receives support, such as where the child sits during a language teaching activity.

Levels of direct intervention

Three levels of direct intervention approaches are differentiated. These are often referred to as 'tiers' or 'waves'.

- The first level includes high quality instruction for all children, for example in a classroom.
- The second level provides intervention for those children who do not benefit sufficiently from the general input all children receive. At this level, additional input is often provided to small groups of children who are offered more opportunities to hear, repeat and use new words. This aims to give children extra practice in using words that have been introduced in the classroom or words that are necessary to access the school curriculum.
- At the third level children receive individual support targeted at each child's specific needs. This may include supporting a child in a specific language area where the child is struggling, such as helping a child to distinguish and produce sounds correctly. Another targeted area might be the correct use of the past tense of irregular verbs, where a child might say, 'He goed to school' instead of 'He went to school'.

Language interventions in the form of programmes provide a structured framework for how language can be facilitated. Programmes generally need to be followed according to the specified content and structure. As Law et al. (2012) summarise: 'A programme is a term used to describe a formalised intervention which is drawn up in such a way that it has key distinctive features which can be replicated' (p.11). In contrast, collections of resources, such as pictures to facilitate vocabulary learning or story cards to improve story telling skills, are not considered programmes (see Chapter 10).

Before choosing any specific language programme it is important to reflect on which programme(s) might be beneficial for an individual child, and why. Five aspects need to be considered when selecting a programme.

1 *Language development is complex and builds on early non-verbal communicative behaviour.* These basic non-verbal skills need to develop first, or simultaneously with language. For example, speech–motor skills, such as the ability to move the lips, tongue, and jaw in order to speak, need to be developed as these skills are crucial for producing speech sounds. Children also need to develop gestures which are used for non-verbal communication, and cognitive skills such as attention and memory which also form a prerequisite for learning processes. For example, if a person picks up a ball and says 'This is a ball', children must be able to do the following:
   - focus their attention on the person who is talking as well as focussing on the object;
   - memorise the word 'ball';
   - make the link that the object the person is holding in their hand is called a 'ball'.

2 *Not all children are the same.* It is important to know a child's language strengths and weaknesses in order to select an appropriate language programme and to adapt it if necessary.

3 *Children's language skills change over time* and show different developmental patterns. Hence, some language programmes may only suit a particular age group or children at a particular stage of development.

4 *The environment* in which a language programme is delivered may impact on its effectiveness. Such factors include: time available to deliver the intervention, space or rooms available, expertise and experience of the person delivering the programme, and what support they receive.

5 *A child may have complex needs*, showing difficulties in other developmental areas such as hearing, motor control or social development. Therefore there needs to be a careful choice or balance between different interventions in order to meet a child's needs. Everyone who is concerned with a child's education or upbringing needs to be involved in this decision.

How do we know whether an intervention programme is useful?

A large variety of programmes are available, targeting different user groups. They vary considerably regarding their structure, teaching strategies and targeted skills. Therefore, a range of factors needs to be considered when choosing or evaluating a programme. Below is a list of questions to ask when looking at a programme. This list is not exhaustive. The questions below act as prompts to help you to think about the different aspects of programme structure and quality.

- Do the authors explain why the intervention programme was developed and how it relates to previous programmes, research and theories concerning language development?
- Is there any scientific evidence/formal evaluation to show that the intervention works? The evidence may vary from a description of the programme and its background to group studies exploring the difference between groups who received and those who did not receive the programme.
- Does the programme address the aims it claims to address? For example, if a programme aims to improve vocabulary, does it include specific activities to promote vocabulary skills?
- Does the intervention programme have some meaning or value for the child? For example does it help a child to communicate better in everyday life?
- Does the programme meet the children's/parent(s)' needs?
- Are the outlined aims of the programme achievable for the child/parent(s)?
- Can the programme be integrated into daily life, for example within the family structures or within the school curriculum?
- For whom is the programme intended?
- Can it be used by different people such as teachers, therapists or parents?
- Is the programme described in enough detail to enable it to be administered?
- Can the programme be used flexibly or does it require a strict adherence to the manual?
- Is specific training needed to administer the programme?
- Is the programme feasible for the intended setting, target group and professionals/parents? Is it feasible considering budget, time constraints, resources and workforce?
- Are all the required materials provided, or are they available in everyday settings?
- Is the material child-friendly and engaging?
- Is the material easy to use?
- Is the material culturally appropriate?

What intervention programmes are currently used and available in the UK?

After reflecting on what to consider when choosing a language programme we need to think about:

a) What aspects of language development can be promoted and how might this be done?
b) What intervention approaches, programmes and manuals currently exist?
c) What is the current evidence base regarding their effectiveness?

As part of a larger governmental initiative a team of researchers was asked to collate information about the language programmes currently in use and to consider how services for children with speech, language and communication needs could be improved (the Better Communication Research Programme (BCRP). For more information see www2.warwick.ac.uk/fac/soc/cedar/better/).

Among the several publications resulting from this project were two *What Works* government reports (Law et al. 2012). These reports include information about the language programmes which are available, in terms of their aims, target groups, target areas, and their current evidence-based evaluation. The *What Works* information continues to be published as an online database which is regularly updated and extended. It is part of the Communication Trust website which also provides a range of resources for parents and practitioners (see www.thecommunicationtrust.org.uk). In addition there are two short videos produced by RALLI (a video-led campaign to raise awareness of language impairments; www.youtube.com/user/RALLIcampaign) in which the BCRP and its findings are described.

In the remainder of this chapter the different language areas that interventions may target are summarised and some examples of interventions are provided.

Law et al. (2012) differentiate three levels of evidence: strong, moderate and indicative evidence.

Strong evidence

For a programme to have strong evidence a systematic review needs to be available. A systematic review requires that different studies have evaluated the programme's effectiveness taking into account all available findings.

Moderate evidence

Moderate evidence is assumed when at least one large study with a comprehensive experimental design has been conducted.

Indicative evidence

Indicative evidence means that the programme addresses the skills it claims to target. Furthermore, it has a comprehensible structure but lacks empirical evidence from research studies about its effectiveness.

Language areas which programmes may address

Attention and listening skills

Attention and listening skills are an essential foundation for the development of children's language and for successful classroom participation. In order to follow instructions and understand stories children need to pay attention to and remember what was said. Although this sounds simple, the ability to actively listen and attend is a complex skill which starts developing from an early age. However, the quantity and quality of opportunities to experience good listening models and learn active listening skills varies among children as they are exposed to different types of listening at home, in an early years setting or at school.

Potential intervention strategies/components

- Encourage children to look at the person who is talking.
- Discuss why it is important to look at and listen to each other.
- Discuss other situations where paying attention and listening are important.
- Praise the desired behaviour, for example when a child shows good listening.
- Make it clear to children what they are expected to do, for example looking at some pictures.
- Make it clear to the children when a task is finished, for example when a story has come to an end.
- Give the children time to look at any materials first before giving instructions. For example, before asking children to retell a story, allow them first to have a look at the book.
- Encourage turn-taking. This means that the children learn when to speak and when to listen to others – for example, by saying 'Now it's Jamelia's turn to tell us what she did at the weekend. Are we all listening?'

Example of an intervention programme with a focus on attention and listening skills: Teaching Children to Listen (Spooner and Woodcock 2010)

This programme is designed to be used in large or small group settings by teachers, teaching assistants or therapists. It aims to teach children four basic listening rules: to sit still; to stay quiet and allow everyone to listen; to listen to all of the words the person who is talking is saying, and to look at the person who is talking (p.7). The manual includes the Listening Skills Rating Scale which evaluates the children's listening level.

The level of evidence regarding this programme at the moment is *indicative* since there are no studies including control groups of children who did not receive intervention while another group was treated with this approach. However, observations of children from thirty-four primary schools in the UK have shown an improvement of listening skills after delivering the programme for six weekly sessions.

Listening comprehension

Listening comprehension includes the ability to understand spoken language such as following instructions, or understanding descriptions or stories. Comprehension might break down because of memory limitations, vocabulary deficits, or problems understanding grammatical structures such as differentiating between singular and plural. Since listening skills are vital for language development, listening comprehension or active listening components are incorporated in various programmes.

Potential intervention strategies/components

- Tell and retell stories, including asking questions about the story.
- Ask children to follow instructions, such as when role playing shopping in a supermarket, selling each other food; or a simulated 'PE lesson' with children giving each other instructions where to run or how to jump.
- Use strategies to increase listening comprehension, for example: using shorter sentences and focussing on the main actions of the story; supporting spoken language with pictures/videos; rephrasing instructions using different words to describe what they are supposed to do.

Examples of intervention programmes with a focus on listening comprehension

Two examples are the Oral Language Programme, a twenty-week intervention for reception-aged children (Bowyer-Crane et al. 2008; Carroll et al. 2011), and the Nuffield Early Language Intervention, a thirty-week oral language intervention delivered in nursery and reception (Fricke et al. 2013, www.ican.org.uk/nuffield).

Both of these target three main components:

- speaking and active listening,
- vocabulary,
- narrative skills.

The interventions are delivered by trained teaching assistants. Comprehensive manuals documenting activities and procedures to promote spoken language, including listening comprehension, are available. Both programmes build on previous interventions and follow established principles for listening, vocabulary, and narrative teaching. They show *moderate* evidence of effectiveness.

Speech

Speech is made up of the sounds we use to talk, whereas language is made up of the actual things we say. We produce speech sounds by using our tongue, lips, soft palate, jaws and teeth. Some children may struggle to coordinate all these to utter sounds, resulting in different types of errors. For example, children may delete sounds from words so that they say 'fog' instead of 'frog', or they may swap sounds, saying 'tup' instead of 'cup'.

Speech difficulties may impact on a child's language skills by reducing their intelligibility, so that a child might know all the words necessary to convey meaning but might not be understood by others due to their incorrect pronunciation of the words.

Potential intervention strategies/components

- Improve listening skills so the child learns to differentiate similar sounds such as /d/ and /g/.
- Practise speech production of specific sounds.
- Work on sequencing sounds.

Example of an intervention programme with a focus on speech: Minimal Pair Contrast (Lancaster and Pope 1989)

The aim is to make children aware of their speech errors by presenting pairs of words containing a minimal sound contrast the child has not mastered yet. For example, if a child is not able to differentiate between the sounds /t/ and /k/ they may not be able to differentiate between the words 'tea' and 'key'. When using the programme the child may be presented with pictures of word pairs such as 'tea and key', 'table and cable' or 'cap and tap'. By making them aware of the different word meanings, awareness of the sound differences is built up and this forms a basis for correct sound production. This type of intervention is usually provided by speech and language therapists. There is *moderate* evidence from a range of studies that this approach is suitable and effective for children with mild and consistent speech difficulties.

Vocabulary

Vocabulary includes all the words a person knows, and comprises different word types such as verbs, nouns and adjectives. Our receptive vocabulary is made up of the words we understand; our expressive vocabulary is made up of the words we are able to produce when speaking or writing. However, we need to differentiate between the number of words known (quantity) and how much is known about one particular word (quality).

The more we know about a word, the better we understand its meaning. We can then use the word in different contexts and be more aware when it is appropriate to use a word and when not. For example, at an early age many children call every animal which has four legs 'dog'. They overgeneralise their knowledge and put everything that fits the criterion of 'four legs' into the same category. With time their understanding of the concept of an actual dog deepens and they understand the different characteristics of a 'dog'. This then allows them to differentiate a dog from other animals such as a cat or a pig.

Potential intervention strategies/components

- Teach age-appropriate words which are part of the school curriculum and the children's everyday experiences.
- Teach a wide range of words, including different word types such as nouns, verbs and adjectives.
- Provide age-appropriate definitions for words to deepen the children's understanding of a word.
- Revise new words as often as possible.
- Encourage links between newly learned words and previously known words.
- Use taught words in different contexts and grammatical structures to deepen children's understanding of the words.
- Provide opportunities to say words aloud and to learn to pronounce them correctly.

Example of an intervention programme with a focus on vocabulary: Strathclyde Language Intervention Programme (Boyle et al. 2007)

This programme is delivered by speech and language therapists or trained and supported teaching assistants. It targets different aspects of spoken language, including narrative, grammar, comprehension monitoring and vocabulary. Vocabulary learning is supported by providing strategies about how to remember words. This might involve thinking about what the word means, what function it may have, how it might be linked to other words and how it sounds.

Children are encouraged to develop their own ways of memorising new words. For example, they are taught how to cue themselves or how to rehearse a word, using it in different contexts. The manual provides a comprehensive description of how to administer the programme and also includes a repository of activities. The evidence level is described as *moderate* since research has shown that children with spoken language difficulties benefit from the intervention.

Grammar (morphology-syntax)

Knowledge about the structure of words (morphology) allows us to understand and build words in their different forms. For example, it allows us to differentiate between singular and plural ('dog' versus 'dogs') or between the present tense and the past tense ('we run' versus 'we ran'). Knowledge about the structure of sentences (syntax) allows us to understand and build sentences. We learn that word order can define meaning, so that for example when we hear a sentence such as 'The girl chases the boy', we are able to understand that the girl is actually running after the boy and not vice versa.

Potential intervention strategies/components

- Provide repeated presentations of different grammatical forms, for example singular and plural forms: 'Here is a cat. Here is another cat. There are two cats.' The child may be prompted to produce the same form by saying 'And look here is a dog, and another dog. We have two ....' This may help the children to identify, remember and use specific grammatical structures such as plurals.
- Provide grammatically correct sentences after an incomplete or incorrect child utterance. For example, a child might say 'Mouse hide,' and the adult might then say 'Yes, the mouse is hiding.' This is intended to direct the child's attention to the correct grammatical form, or a more advanced utterance, and allows the child to compare immediately their own production with that of the adult.
- Highlight relations within sentences by stressing specific parts – for example, 'The boy likes his teddy. The girl likes her ball.'
- Provide visual cues using shapes or colours to teach grammatical rules explicitly. Specific parts of a sentence may be colour-coded to highlight word classes, so that, for example, all action words will be the same colour.

Example of an intervention programme with a focus on grammar: Shape coding (Ebbels 2007)

This programme builds on earlier work such as that of Lea (1970), adapting the principles of using colour- and shape-coding to teach grammatical rules. Parts of speech are marked with colours, phrases are marked with shapes and timelines with arrows to indicate verb tenses. It was originally designed for school-aged children, primarily in key stages 2 and 3, who have specific language impairments. It can be delivered by teachers and speech and language therapists. The evidence level is *moderate* and suggests that children with spoken language difficulties may benefit from the intervention. For more information about the programme see www.moorhouse.surrey.sch.uk/shape-coding-course

Narratives

Narratives include a child's ability to tell a story by sequencing and structuring a story or recounting personal events. To do this a child needs to know the characters and events, to be able to pick out the most relevant aspects of the story, to put the events in a logical order, and to understand cause and effect relationships.

Potential intervention strategies/components

- Choose a variety of stories or events which children can relate to their everyday lives, such as missing the bus.
- Speak about the key elements of the story – for example, talk about specific words and what they mean, and discuss the main characters and events of the story.
- Sequence the events of the story. The narrative may also take the form of instructions which can then be sequenced. For example: 'When we make a salad we need to use a chopping board, bowl and knife. We wash the tomatoes, put them on the board, cut them up with the knife and then put them in the bowl.'
- Support stories/instructions with pictures and 'wh-' question cards – 'who, where, when and why'.
- Act out parts of the story/instructions.
- In a story, talk about how the characters might feel and what might happen next.
- Talk about the children's own life experience in relation to the story.

Example of an intervention programme with a focus on narratives: the Becky Shanks Narrative Intervention (Shanks 2011)

This intervention provides a manual for teachers, therapists or assistants to teach children the main components of a story. Stories have a beginning, middle and end and it is important for them to know who is part of the story, where the story is taking place and when. The programme targets children in key stage 1 and the material can be used in small group or whole classroom settings.

The level of difficulties for stories can be varied. The children are encouraged to answer questions about the story and also to tell their own stories. Materials such as picture cards are provided to support learning. There is general evidence that narrative intervention is successful and some *indicative* evidence exists for this specific approach that children with language difficulties improve their narrative skills.

Pragmatics

Pragmatic skills include the ability to understand the social functions of language. For example, we need pragmatic skills to understand jokes, to know when to be silent or when to provide an explanation. We also learn what words and which language style to use in different situations. For example, the language we use when we are with friends differs from the language we use at work or at school. One component of pragmatics is the ability to recognise if we have or have not understood something and to use strategies to overcome our lack of understanding. For example, when we hear a word for the first time we identify it as a word we have not heard before and that we consequently do not understand. We can respond to this comprehension difficulty by asking someone what it means. This ability to respond actively to comprehension problems is a crucial skill when learning language. It is also important in sustaining communication.

Potential intervention strategies/components

- Explain which language/words to use in specific settings/situations.
- Provide role plays to practise different uses of language.
- Teach children that it is all right to ask for help.
- Provide an environment in which children feel confident to express their misunderstanding.
- Teach specific strategies to signal comprehension problems.

Example of an intervention programme with a focus on pragmatics: Social Communication Intervention Programme (Adams et al. 2012)

This programme aims to help children with pragmatic and social communication difficulties. It targets three key areas. (p.250):

1 language processing – e.g. activities to understand and use non-literal language;
2 pragmatics – e.g. activities to enhance turn-taking skills;
3 social understanding and social interaction – e.g. activities to understand the thoughts and intentions of others.

The programme was evaluated in primary school settings and is intended to be delivered three times a week in individual sessions by a specialist or trained assistants. The evidence level is *moderate*.

Phonological awareness and letter-sound knowledge

Phonological awareness is the ability to understand and manipulate sounds in words independent of their meaning. These skills include, for example, the ability to decide how many syllables are in a word, the ability to spot rhymes and the ability to identify words which start with the same sound.

Knowledge about a word's structure can be used to learn and remember words. For example, children need to learn strategies to store and retrieve a word, including remembering sound similarities and differences in relation to other words, or remembering the length of words or the number of syllables. Letter-sound knowledge which requires a child to know the sound of a letter is linked to phonological awareness development and literacy skills. Therefore, although those two skills do not fall under the category *language skills* as such, many pre-school- and school-based language intervention programmes include phonological awareness and letter-sound knowledge activities. It is also important to consider that once children are able to read they use these literacy competences to expand their vocabulary and grammar skills.

Potential intervention strategies/components

• Raise awareness of the word form of words independent of their meaning.
• Use multisensory methods which may include activities that allow the use of different senses. For example, to raise children's awareness of syllables you could clap the syllables of a word, jump three times for a three-syllabic word, cut up pictures such as 'crocodile' into three parts (cro-co-dile), or move one building block for each syllable.

- Use familiar songs and counting-out rhymes to explain the concept of syllables, rhymes and sounds.

Example of an intervention programme with a focus on phonological awareness and letter-sound knowledge: the Gillon Phonological Awareness Programme (Gillon 2008)

This includes activities to promote phonological awareness, speech production, and early literacy skills in children around the age of five to seven years who have speech difficulties. The phonological awareness activities are delivered in individual sessions provided by speech and language therapists. They include rhyme and sound tasks which are linked to letter-sound knowledge practice to promote the link between sounds and written language. The manual and resources are free and are available for downloading (see www.education.canterbury.ac.nz/people/gillon/gillon_phonological_awareness_training_programme.shtml). The level of evidence is *moderate*. Two studies confirmed that the intervention improved the phonological awareness and literacy skills of children aged five to seven years with speech difficulties, and that this improvement persisted over time. A third study showed that the programme could also be delivered successfully to a group of three to four year olds.

Link between spoken and written language

Spoken language is a crucial component for successful literacy development. Learning to read, that is translating written letters into speech sounds, largely depends on phonological awareness and letter-sound knowledge. However, the ability to understand written text (reading comprehension) relies on spoken language skills such as vocabulary, grammar and narrative skills. For further information about current literacy interventions see the Dyslexia-SpLD Trust website (www.thedyslexia-spldtrust.org.uk/). The website provides a large repository of information for parents and practitioners, including the 'What works for children and young people with literacy difficulties?' report by Brooks (2013).

Language programmes for children for whom English is an additional language (EAL)

Across the UK, many children are growing up speaking a language other than English at home. In England, 18.1 per cent of primary school pupils are learning English as an additional language (EAL; DfE 2013). Although growing up with more than one language does not in itself cause language difficulties, some children with EAL may need early support to reach adequate levels of proficiency in the language of instruction (Tickell 2011). For a short overview of issues around bilingualism see the following RALLI videos: Introduction to Bilingualism: Dispelling the Myths www.youtube. com/watch?v=p9iWG0M5z40 and/or Bilingualism and Specific Language Impairment www.youtube.com/watch?v=g7Sj_uRV7S4.

If a child speaks more than one language it is important to consider how much they hear and speak each language in their everyday lives. The features and characteristics of each language also need to be taken into account. For example, not all sounds exist in all languages and a child needs to learn which sounds to use in which language. Moreover, cultural differences might influence how children learn languages, for example how adults and children interact with each other.

It is important to know children's language competences in all the languages they learn in order to understand whether a child has limited English language skills due to limited exposure to English in his/her environment or due to language learning difficulties. However, this has proven to be a difficult task since standardised assessments are not available in all children's home languages. Although translated or adapted assessments are often used, these do not take account of cultural and linguistic differences between languages or the varying levels of multilingualism among the professionals administering them. Thus it is difficult for speech and language therapists, teachers and other educational/health professionals to identify multilingual children who have general language learning difficulties as opposed to specific difficulties learning a new language.

This also makes it difficult to choose appropriate interventions for children with EAL. A decision has to be made regarding whether a child would benefit from a small-group language support programme or whether they are in need of specific intervention by a speech and language therapist.

When delivering intervention to a group of children with EAL, it is important to know about the similarities and differences between the languages the children are learning, such as whether some grammatical rules are shared, and to understand any cultural differences of how language is acquired within the family/community. Another aspect is to consider how both languages can be used to facilitate language acquisition in general. This may include deciding when and to what extent each language should be used in specific language activities and daily life. Moreover, it is crucial to think about language features in all languages a child speaks and how these may influence each other. For instance, the rules and characteristics of one language may make it easier, or harder, to learn aspects of another language.

In recent years a growing number of interventions have been developed specifically to support children with EAL. However, there is limited evidence to show that language programmes for children with EAL are effective (Thordardottir 2010). This might be related to specific issues regarding intervention for children with EAL. Children with EAL form a diverse group due to various language combinations, language experiences and cultural backgrounds. Therefore, more research is clearly needed in this comparably young area of language interventions to shed more light on what works for whom and why.

Parent-based language intervention programmes

Language development is not an isolated process but includes everyone and everything that surrounds a child, including parents, wider family, friends, early years workers and teachers. Within this natural environment everyday talk shapes a child's communication skills. Children imitate interactional strategies and adapt to their communication partners. Hence, parents who spend a lot of time with their children and who know their children's behaviour and skills best are important agents in providing adequate linguistic input and facilitating language learning. Components which play a role are:

- the quantity and quality of what parents say;
- how much parents interact with their children;
- how parents respond to what their child says and does;
- how parents help their children to acquire language;
- what home environment they provide, including, for example, the number of books available to a child.

Therefore it is important to involve parents actively in language intervention programmes. They may be the ones who deliver the intervention, or parts of it. This involvement may not only raise parents' motivation to work with their child, but may also provide support for them, for example, through parent training sessions, thus enhancing the communication between parents and educators.

Evidence for the effectiveness of parental involvement is mixed, but it generally shows a disappointing picture based on current research. Although Roberts and Kaiser's meta-analysis of studies (2011) showed that parent-implemented language intervention improves spoken language skills in typically developing children and children with spoken language problems, a recent review commissioned by the Nuffield Foundation came to a less positive conclusion (See and Gorard 2013). Further research is needed to explore the type of parent involvement and training that is most effective.

Potential intervention strategies/components

- Instruct parents at home in order to train interaction and teach techniques in their familiar environment.
- Raise awareness of how daily activities such as 'face washing' can be verbalised. 'You take some soap and wash your face. You wash your

right cheek, your left cheek, then you wash both cheeks. After that you wash your chin, and at the end you wash your nose...'

- Teach parents techniques about how they can increase verbal interaction with their children during play or daily routines. 'It's cold outside. What will you wear – a tee shirt or a jumper?'
- Discuss ways in which children's utterances can be expanded. For example, the child says 'Juice'; the adult says 'There is juice. Do you want some juice? I'll pour you a glass of juice.'

Example of an intervention programme with a focus on parent involvement: It Takes Two to Talk® – The Hanen Program® for Parents of Children with Language Delays (Pennington and Thomson 2007)

Hanen offers a range of intervention programmes, primarily for parents, to facilitate language and communication in children with language difficulties (see www.hanen.org). Certified speech and language therapists provide training to parents that includes teaching sessions and home visits. Parents are videoed while interacting with their children. Parents receive individual feedback from other parents and the course instructor on their behaviour. They also discuss different techniques for how to improve communication with their children. The training is supported by a guidebook. The evidence level is *moderate* – a range of studies have been conducted, showing positive effects on children with language difficulties.

Language intervention programmes for children with ASD

As outlined in Chapter 8, Autism Spectrum Disorder is a term used to describe a group of neurodevelopmental disorders. These children display a range of symptoms in the areas of social communication, behaviour, interaction, and language development. They may show attention difficulties, anxiety, and repetitive and challenging behaviours. Symptoms vary considerably and may range from mild to severe. Therefore it is still under debate how to detect ASD correctly, how to define subgroups, and how to decide which therapy is most suitable for each child (Camarata 2014). As summarised in a review by Warren et al. (2011), the majority of intervention studies published so far have shown a weak evidence base. Since children with ASD may show different types of symptoms, often a combination of therapies is selected.

Generally five subgroups of intervention approaches can be differentiated:

- medical;
- behavioural;
- educational;

- allied health interventions (including speech and language therapy);
- complementary and alternative medicine interventions.

Medical intervention

There is research evidence that some medication can reduce repetitive and challenging behaviour such as aggression, hyperactivity and self-injury. However, these medicines are associated with side effects such as weight gain or sleepiness and should therefore be used with caution (Warren et al. 2011). The evidence base for potential risks or benefits of different medicines needs to be carefully considered and discussed with the doctors involved.

Behavioural intervention

Behavioural interventions include a range of different approaches. Warren et al. (2011 p.19) summarise the following broad categories:

- early intensive behavioural and developmental approaches;
- social skills approaches;
- play-/interaction-based approaches;
- interventions focussed on behaviour commonly associated with ASD;
- other general behavioural approaches.

Focussed intervention programmes aim to facilitate a specific change in behaviour or development. These focussed interventions are delivered in a relatively short period of time (Odom et al. 2010). In contrast, comprehensive treatment models include different components, are very time intensive, and are administered over a long period of time. Examples of some established comprehensive treatment models are the Lovaas Model (Lovaas 1987), the Denver Model (Dawson et al. 2010), the Walden Early Childhood Program (McGee et al. 2001) and Pivotal Response Treatment (Koegel and Koegel 2012). Warren et al. (2011) state that there is some evidence that early intensive behavioural and developmental interventions are effective in improving cognitive skills, language development, and adaptive behaviour.

Educational intervention

Educational intervention programmes are provided in early years or school settings and aim to improve children's independence, academic achievement and behaviour in the classroom. Children may receive individual instruction and support. One element is to structure everyday activities, introducing routines and providing a consistent setting. In addition, visual support may be used to support communication and learning – for example, the Picture Exchange Communication System (PECS; see Chapter 8).

Allied health interventions (e.g. speech and language intervention)

This category includes a broad range of interventions, including, for example, sensory or auditory integration and speech and language therapy. Since communication difficulties are core symptoms of ASD, speech and language interventions play an important role in the treatment of ASD.

Complementary and alternative medicine intervention

This group of interventions includes, for example, massage or acupuncture. The evidence base for their use in the treatment of ASD is very limited and more studies are needed to evaluate their effectiveness and any side effects they may have (Warren et al. 2011).

Advances in technology

Recent advances in technology have led to new ways of treating children with language difficulties. A range of digital programmes is now available that can support learning, including computer-based programmes, e-books and apps for tablets and smartphones. They may increase children's motivation, provide instant feedback on tasks, and offer repeated opportunities to practise target behaviour. However, it is important to consider the same questions as when evaluating language programmes.

The majority of electronic resources lack empirical evidence. Moreover, they often have limited flexibility in order to target children's specific needs and do not provide the individual feedback which can be offered by a specifically trained teaching assistant. Therefore, electronic devices and programmes may supplement a language intervention. However, in most cases they are unlikely to replace human interaction and children should be supervised when using such programmes. New developments in technology and computer-based interventions to support language may have potential, but need to be carefully selected and evaluated.

Summary

There is an increasing knowledge base about how to support children's language development and what intervention strategies work best and for whom. However, we can never be sure about the effectiveness of a language intervention programme for a specific group of children unless it has been rigorously evaluated in a number of studies. It is therefore important to critically appraise the most recent evidence base for new and established intervention programmes as well as consulting relevant professionals.

References

Adams, C., Lockton, E., Gaile, J., Earl, G. and Freed, J. (2012) Implementation of a manualized communication intervention for school-aged children with pragmatic and social communication needs in a randomized controlled trial: The Social Communication Intervention Project. *International Journal of Language and Communication Disorders*, **47** (3), 245–256.

Bowyer-Crane, C., Snowling, M., Duff, F.J., Fieldsend, E., Carroll, J.M. , Miles, J., Goetz, K. and Hulme, C. (2008) Improving early language and literacy skills: Differential effects of an oral language versus a phonology with reading intervention. *Journal of Child Psychology and Psychiatry*, **49** (4), 422–432.

Boyle, J., McCartney, E., Forbes, J. and O'Hare, A. (2007) *Language Therapy Manual: Health technology assessment*. Strathclyde: University of Strathclyde.

Brooks, G. (2013) *What works for children and young people with literacy difficulties?* Bracknell, Berkshire: The Dyslexia-SpLD Trust (www.interventionsforliteracy.org.uk/widgets_GregBrooks/What_works_for_children_fourth_ed.pdf).

Camarata, S. (2014) Early identification and early intervention in autism spectrum disorders: Accurate and effective? *International Journal of Speech-Language Pathology*, **16** (1), 1–10.

Carroll, J.M., Bowyer-Crane, C., Duff, F., Snowling, M.J. and Hulme, C. (2011) *Developing Language and Literacy: Effective Intervention in the Early Years*. Chichester: Wiley-Blackwell.

Dawson G., Rogers S., Munson J., Smith M., Jamie W. et al. (2010) Randomized controlled trial of the Early Start Denver Model: A developmental behavioral intervention for toddlers with autism. Effects on IQ, adaptive behavior, and autism diagnosis. *Pediatrics*, **125** (1), e17–23.

Department of Education (2013) *Statistical First Release: Schools, pupils, and their characteristics*. London: DfE.

Ebbels, S. (2007) Teaching grammar to school-aged children with specific language impairment using Shape Coding. *Child Language Teaching and Therapy*, **23**, 67–93.

Fricke, S., Bowyer-Crane, C., Haley, A.J., Hulme, C. and Snowling, M.J. (2013) Efficacy of language intervention in the early years. *Journal of Child Psychology and Psychiatry and Allied Disciplines*, **54** (3), 280–290.

Gillon, G. (2008) *The Gillon Phonological Awareness Training Programme: An intervention programme for children at risk for reading disorder*. Christchurch: University of Canterbury.

Koegel, R.L. and Koegel, L.K. (2012) *The PRT Pocket Guide: Pivotal response treatment for autism spectrum disorder*. Baltimore, MD: Paul H. Brooks Publishing.

Lancaster, G. and Pope, L. (1989) *Working with Children's Phonology*. Bicester: Winslow.

Law, J., Lee, W., Roulstone, S., Wren, Y., Zeng, B. and Lindsay, G. (2012) '*What Works': Interventions for children and young people with speech, language and communication needs*. London: DfE.

Law, J., Lee, W., Roulstone, S., Wren, Y., Zeng, B. and Lindsay, G. (2012) www. gov.uk/government/publications/what-works-interventions-for-children-and-young-people-with-speech-language-and-communication-needs.

Lea, J. (1970) *The Colour Pattern Scheme: A method of remedial language teaching.* Hurst Green, Surrey, UK: Moor House School.

Lovaas, O.I. (1987) Behavioural treatment and normal, educational and intellectual functioning in young autistic children. *Journal of Consulting and Clinical Psychology,* 55 (1), 3–9 www.lovaas.com.

McGee, G.G., Daly T. and Morrier M.J. (2001) Walden Early Childhood Program. In J.S. Handleman and S.L. Harris (Eds.) *Preschool Education Programs for Children with Autism* (2nd edition) (pp 157–190). Austin, TX: Pro-Ed.

Odom, S.L., Boyd, B.A., Hall, L.J. and Hume, K. (2010) Evaluation of comprehensive treatment models for individuals with autism spectrum disorders. *Journal of Autism and Other Developmental Disorders,* 40 (4), 425–436.

Pennington, L. and Thomson, K. (2007) It Takes Two to Talk® – The Hanen Program® and families of children with motor disorders: A UK perspective. *Child: Care Health and Development,* 33, 691–702.

Roberts, M.Y. and Kaiser, A.P. (2011) The effectiveness of parent-implemented language interventions: A meta-analysis. *American Journal of Speech-Language Pathology,* 20, 180–199.

See, B.H. and Gorard, S. (2013) *What Do Rigorous Evaluations Tell Us About the Most Promising Parental Involvement Interventions? A critical review of what works for disadvantaged children in different age groups.* London: Nuffield Foundation.

Shanks, B. (2011) *Speaking and Listening Through Narrative.* Keighley: Black Sheep Press.

Spooner, L. and Woodcock, J. (2010) *Teaching Children to Listen: A Practical Approach to Developing Children's Listening Skills.* London: Continuum International Publishing Group.

Thordardottir, E. (2010) Towards evidence-based practice in language intervention for bilingual children. *Journal of Communication Disorders,* 43 (6), 523–537.

Tickell, C. (2011) *The Early Years Foundation Stage (EYFS) Review – Report on the Evidence.* London: DfE.

Warren, Z., Veenstra-VanderWeele, J., Stone, W., Bruzek, J.L., Nahmias, A.S., Foss-Feig, J.H. and McPheeters, M.L. (2011) *Therapies for Children With Autism Spectrum Disorders: Comparative effectiveness review No. 26. (Prepared by the Vanderbilt Evidence-based Practice Center under Contract No. 290-2007-10065-1.)* Rockville, MD: Agency for Healthcare Research and Quality.

Further reading

Beck, I.L., McKeown, M.G. and Kucan, L. (2013) *Bringing Words to Life: Robust vocabulary instruction* (2nd edition). New York, London: The Guildford Press.

Carroll, J.M., Bowyer-Crane, C., Duff, F.J., Hulme, C.J. and Snowling, M.J. (2011) *Developing Language and Literacy: Effective intervention in the early years.* Oxford: Wiley-Blackwell.

Nutbrown, C., Hannon, P. and Morgan, A. (2005) *Early Literacy Work with Families: Research, policy and practice*. London: Sage.

Useful weblinks

ICAN (www.ican.org.uk): A charity which aims to help children with communication difficulties. They offer a large range of services, including the provision of help and advice to parents and practitioners about spoken language difficulties. ICAN also runs the **Talking Point** website (www.talkingpoint.org.uk) which provides information, links and resources for people who work with children but also for parents and children.

RALLI campaign (Raise Awareness of Language Learning Impairment, www.youtube.com/rallicampaign): Provides a large range of videos for different interest groups, including parents, explaining what language impairment is, the impact it may have on children, adolescents and adults, and how children can be supported.

The Communication Trust (www.thecommunicationtrust.org.uk): A consortium of almost fifty voluntary and community service organisations which all have expertise in children's speech, language and communication.

Chapter 10

Supporting young children with speech, language and communication needs

Myra Kersner and Jannet A. Wright

Introduction

The aim of any language work with children with speech, language and communication needs (SLCN) is to help them attain a more acceptable level of language and communication skills for their age. It is important for anyone spending time with such children to encourage language development, and this can be done most effectively as part of their daily routines when they are in familiar and naturalistic settings. The activities suggested in this chapter can be adapted and developed for use in the classroom, early years setting or at home, and can be used by parents or extended family members as well as by professionals.

The ideas offered may be used with any children as they develop speech, language and communication skills, although they will be particularly useful for children with SLCN. In addition, many of the activities may be helpful where children are learning English as an Additional Language (EAL), for example in pre-school settings. With such children it would also be important to ascertain if they are having difficulty with the other language(s) used in the home. If their language skills in their mother tongue are not at the level expected for their age, then this may indicate some possible underlying difficulties which would need to be assessed by a speech and language therapist.

For those working in early years or school settings the suggestions in this chapter can be used alongside any government recommendations and any developments or instructions issued by local authorities about enhancing speech, language and communication development.

When children appear to be having communication difficulties it is useful if early years practitioners and parents can work together to record some details about how the child communicates. If they are able to identify what the child can do and in which areas of communication the child is having difficulties, this will help the speech and language therapist to design appropriate activities or a specific programme that will enable the child to improve and progress. The child's behaviour at home and in nursery or school as well as their performance in physical and social activities should all be noted, as these will help to form a clearer picture of their overall abilities.

In childcare settings, early years practitioners have a number of important roles to play when faced with children with communication difficulties. They will often be the first ones to notice problems while they are working with the children. They will note if a child's behaviour is different from the others within the group – for example, if the child has difficulty following instructions, taking turns or listening to other children. They may be the ones who are in an optimum position to provide a sensitive environment for encouraging language development, and they also have a key role to play in implementing strategies and programmes that may be recommended by a speech and language therapist. They would work with parents and liaise with other professionals such as the speech and language therapist about the child's progress, and may be called upon to monitor whether the child is using their new skills within the childcare environment.

How these roles are performed will be influenced by how the early years workers view language and communication, and their understanding of the stages of normal language development and how language is acquired. The speech and language therapist will provide direction and support, but it is the early years workers who can ensure that children make maximum progress by providing the optimum conditions and opportunities for encouraging communication (see ideas in the book by Gross, 2013).

Language programmes

The term 'language programme' is often used by those working with children with communication difficulties, and yet it may be used in a different way by each person. For example, there are the formalised published programmes such as those referred to in Chapter 9, and there are informal language programmes which are speech and language work schedules designed for individual children. The term language programme may refer to any structured framework which has been devised for the specific purpose of encouraging and teaching speech, language and communication based on the careful assessment of individual children. A language programme will often be designed and/or implemented by any combination of speech and language therapist, early years worker, teacher, assistant or parent.

Any language programme should include the identification of specific language areas that need work. This may be in the area of comprehension or expression, including vocabulary, grammar/syntax and the use of language. The programme should include suggestions about how this work may be fitted into the child's daily routine. Ideally the language areas, and specific items selected within them, should be those which will have maximum impact on the child's ability to influence and understand those around them.

For example, in the case of a non-verbal child (who is not using speech) it may be advisable not to teach long lists of 'things' or object names (nouns). If a smaller selection of these words were taught together with a number of 'event' or 'action' words (verbs), such as 'do, go, make, be', the child would be able to combine two or more words to make simple sentences such as 'Mummy go', 'Need drink', 'Mummy make drink'.

It is important that the content of the activities and the way they are introduced should be adapted to the level of each child's language. Encouragement of language does not have to be restricted to set times and set tasks as it is important to talk to the child and model language in as many different situations as possible. It must be remembered that in order for language work to be beneficial it needs to become part of, and have an effect on, the child's daily routine, and so the activities can take place at home and/or in an early years setting or classroom. However, it may also be necessary to set aside special sessions in order to work on some more formalised language programmes or some specific aspects of language, as outlined in Chapter 9.

Levels of skills

In order for a child to take part in any kind of conversation, different levels of skills need to be in place. For example, the child needs to have the ability to:

1   pay attention to the other person;
2   listen to and hear the words;
3   process and understand the words to make sense of what has been heard;
4   have the appropriate words and language in mind to respond;
5   have the physical ability to form the words in order to respond.

If the child does not have the first level of skill and is not able to pay attention to the other person, or to hear the words and process them, then responding appropriately is going to be more difficult. So, for example, it may be necessary with some children to work on their earlier skills such as listening and attention in order for later language work to be successful. In an early years setting this may necessitate the child being withdrawn temporarily from a group activity in order to work on these skills individually with an adult. Once the child has been able to develop these early skills they may then become a more effective member of the group and may be ready to learn the next aspects of language.

Choosing the right level of activity

Some activities are more complex than others, either because a high level of proficiency is required, or because a number of different skills are involved in one activity.

It is important to look carefully at the skills needed by children in any activity. In the same way as they need to establish pre-language skills in order to develop language, so they need to have the ability to achieve each stage of an activity if they are to succeed with the whole task.

What might appear to be a simple task to an adult, or even an older child, may involve sets of skills which have developed over years, enabling them to perform the task almost automatically. For example, a popular activity when helping children to improve their attention and listening is to match a sound to a picture so that the picture becomes associated with the sound. For example, a ball may be matched to the sound /b/ and a tap may be matched to the sound /t/. This matching can be done for all the sounds of English. Children may be given several picture cards – for example, depicting taps and balls. When they hear the adult make a sound such as /b/ or /t/ they are expected to identify the appropriate picture.

This would be an easy task for an adult, but young children will find it more difficult. Adults may approach this task in two ways.

1   Learn by heart the sounds that are associated with each picture.
2   Use the learned ability to separate the sounds in the word (phonic skills) into /t-a-p/ to work out that the sound being represented by the picture 'tap' is /t/.

Young children are less able to do this task as they have fewer resources available. They are unlikely to have phonic skills, which are associated with reading; also their ability to remember information is limited. Thus the child's failure to perform the task may be due to limited memory, rather than an inability to distinguish between sounds.

For example, if a child is told to 'Wash the doll's face', this involves at least three different levels of skill. In order to carry out this instruction, the child has to be able to:

1   listen to the speaker;
2   understand and remember the words;
3   carry out the task by picking up the doll and washing its face.

The number of skills required to complete a task must be considered. For example, children may find it difficult to build something with LEGO or bricks while following the adult's instructions, as they have to divide their attention between the speaker and the task. When asked to complete such a task, children who have poor hand control will find it even more difficult, as they are less able to give their full attention to the instructions. It may be easier for them if the instructions were split up into small chunks, the first given before they begin the task. The instructions could be, for example: 'Pick up the doll; pour water into the bowl; dip the face cloth into the water; squeeze out the extra water; wash the doll's face.' Each additional instruction should be given only when the adult has the child's full attention.

Activities to encourage language

Each child is unique. Children with speech, language and communication needs will require strategies tailored to meet their individual difficulties, needs and interests to help them overcome their difficulties. In addition, they need to experience how language is used in daily activities, to hear it, to understand it and to learn how to take part in everyday conversations. It should be possible to combine these routine activities with specific strategies. Any language programme that has been specifically designed for an individual child can be supplemented by classroom and home activities which encourage conversation and which will help to develop underlying language skills.

In an early years setting, for example, it may be useful and time saving to collect activities that have been enjoyed by the child and store them in a box. These may include some commercially available material as well as activities devised by the staff. For example, they could include games that:

- develop the child's knowledge of the world in specific areas such as colours and size;
- help the child to listen to spoken commands;
- help the child to remember spoken commands;
- help the child to follow a short story.

The box may therefore include such items as pictures, objects or sequencing cards that relate to the short story, dolls/teddies, a small table and chairs or a doll's cot, small cups and spoons. Then commands could be given such as, 'Put the dolly in the bed', 'Put the teddy on the chair', 'Give the dolly a drink'.

The child's current language abilities will influence the choice of activity. The activities could be organised according to their level of difficulty so that easier tasks would be introduced first and harder ones presented only when the child has the necessary skills to progress.

For example, when listening to speech sounds it is easier for a child to distinguish between large differences in sounds and words, such as the difference between 'coat' and 'letter', before moving on to the harder task of choosing between words which sound very similar, such as 'coat' and 'goat'.

It is hard to hear the difference between two words which differ in only one sound. These are the minimal pairs as referred to in Chapter 4. Another example of a minimal pair is 'car' and 'tar'– two words that also differ by only one sound.

So, when pictures are presented where the two words which the child has to choose between sound completely different, as in 'coat – letter', and the adult says 'Show me the coat', it is comparatively easy for the child to pick out the word 'coat' when it is being contrasted with the word 'letter'. The task is harder if the adult says 'Show me the coat', and the pair of words that the child has to choose between is 'coat – goat'. In this example, if the child has any difficulties with hearing this could be a significant factor. If the child cannot pick out the word 'coat' when paired with 'letter' it is unlikely that s/he would be able to pick out the word 'coat' from the pair 'coat – goat'.

Language tasks may be presented using the real articles where practical, or more often they will be represented by miniature toys or in picture, spoken or written form. Use can be made of books, commercial materials, toys, computer graphics and everyday objects, so long as the message is clear and the child's interest is captured.

Ways of responding

Children's levels of functioning are affected by the way in which adults respond to and communicate with them. At home a conversation between a parent and child is usually two-way, but in a nursery/classroom setting a conversation between an early years worker/teacher and a child may be one-sided, with the adult, doing all the talking.

Practitioners who want to try and change this pattern could listen to a recording of themselves talking to the children or ask a colleague to write down what they say (see Chapter 5). This may help them to gain insight into the way they talk and listen in a conversation. One area it will highlight is the time given to children to respond to a comment or question from them. Often adults rush a conversational exchange with children and do not give them time to organise their thoughts and respond verbally.

In an early years setting, if time can be consistently found for one adult to play with and talk to a child, communication is likely to become more rewarding. By communicating one-to-one with the same person who is not a member of the child's family, that child can gain confidence. Such one-to-one situations provide opportunities for both the adult and child to adapt to one another's behaviour and style of speaking.

When parents and professionals are talking to children, especially children with SLCN, they need to limit what they say, slow their speech down and leave longer than normal pauses between turns so that the child has time to understand and process what has been said and put together a reply. Adults may have to start the conversation which will, ideally, arise from an activity or object that holds the attention of both the adult and child. Then, the adult will encourage the exchange of ideas by prompting the child to communicate again.

However, the contributions made to the conversation should be balanced, so the child must be encouraged or allowed to take the lead at times (see Chapter 5). Children need the opportunity to introduce topics for conversation, and to ask questions and respond to them, as soon as they are able. They are less likely to contribute if the adults continually adopt a controlling role and ask a great number of questions. This situation can arise when adults are busy, especially if children appear to offer little or their contributions are unintelligible. As children's language develops and they practise using their new skills it should be easier to have a conversation with them and to see them as equal partners.

It should be remembered that children who have difficulty producing words are still capable of communicating. Responses should be made to any attempts at communication, which for some children might involve gaze direction, hand pointing, body position and occasional vocalisations instead of words. These cues often are unclear and may be misinterpreted at times, but at least they give some idea of the child's interests and desire to communicate. Adults will need to use non-verbal responses, such as gesture and facial expression, to support their speech when responding to such children. This may help them understand and may encourage the children to use more gestures and facial expressions themselves in order to be understood. For example, this could involve exaggerating facial expressions of happiness, regret or sadness when telling a story, or sounding and looking particularly animated or excited at different parts of the story in order to grab the child's attention. The use of such animation will also underline the meaning of the words and may help a struggling child to understand. In the same way gestures may be added, such as pointing or hands on the face to indicate shock, as these may help with comprehension.

Early language encouragement

One of the most natural ways in which children learn to use language is through nursery rhymes, simple songs such as 'The Wheels on the Bus', or universal finger games such as the illustration of the birds Peter and Paul who are sitting on the wall. The constant repetition of words and phrases that occurs in these activities provides excellent practice for speech and language. Even children who have difficulty forming their own words and sentences can usually achieve instant success supplying the missing word at the end of a familiar line of a song or rhyme. These activities provide useful examples of turn taking, and opportunities for practising vocabulary that can be built gradually from one word upwards. This is particularly helpful for children for whom English is an additional language. The repetition enables them to join in quickly and so build their English vocabulary.

How to ensure progress

The aim of encouraging language development is to enable children to use their communication skills to have an effect on the environment. They need to be given the kind of words that can make things happen for them. For example, if they want a drink they need to learn to be able to ask for some juice, milk, tea, or whatever they like to drink. Learning lists of words, phrases and sentences may not be helpful as they are unlikely to be used outside the taught situation. What is required is to build on the skills they already have, skills that have already been observed and identified, and to help them to learn words, phrases and sentences that are important and meaningful to them.

Children acquire language by identifying the rules that operate in their language from the examples presented to them. From these examples they may make their own sentences which can be used in new situations. Children may overuse certain new rules as explained in Chapters 2 and 9, but it is important to recognise this as a part of the learning process. For example, many children understand that adding 'ed' makes the past tense such as 'walk, walked'. But then they will also say 'I goed' rather than 'I went', or 'I runned' instead of 'I ran'. Clear examples and repetition of the same situations increase the likelihood of connections being made between the words and the grammatical rules.

If children are to acquire and use the language they hear within a classroom in new situations, then it must reflect the language of their educational environment. Although there may be different cultural influences if English is not their first language, in order to function in an educational group setting they must be taught how to respond in everyday English speech. For example, if a child is shown a picture of a woman cooking and asked what the woman is doing, the most natural response would be 'Cooking', rather than a full sentence such as 'The woman is cooking'.

Modelling and extending

As explained in Chapter 2, modelling occurs spontaneously between an adult and a child when the child is acquiring language. If a child is having difficulties learning to talk, then this strategy of modelling may be used to improve and extend what the child says. Thus, the listener uses the child's utterance and takes it one stage further, using the same form but adding to its length and complexity as in the example below.

> Child: 'Cat eat.'
> Adult: 'The cat is eating.'
> Child: 'Cat eating.'
> Adult: 'The cat is eating some fish.'

It may be possible to use modelling to create a new sentence while maintaining the topic, as in the next example.

Child: 'The man is shopping.'
Adult: 'Yes, he has bought a shirt '
Child: 'Look, money.'
Adult: 'He will have to give the lady some money for the shirt.'

The use of questions

Every effort should be made to use language to convey an appropriate message. It is best to avoid asking children display questions, where the child knows that the speaker already has the answer. For example, a mother might ask, 'What colour pencil is this?' but the child realises that the mother knows the answer because she is looking at the pencil. It would be more appropriate for the mother to ask the same question when only the child can see the object and she cannot. Another common display question is to ask a child, with a picture on the front of their t-shirt or jumper, 'What's that on the front of your jumper?' The child knows the adult can see it, probably more easily than they can themselves, and so they may ignore the question.

It is not always helpful if adults try to encourage children to use their language by asking them lots of questions, because questions are controlling and demanding. In the classroom when teachers ask questions children tend to answer them, but they do not add anything to the conversation. Children contribute more and produce longer utterances when fewer questions are used in the conversation. So, children may be encouraged to make more contributions if adults talk about their own experiences and/or comment on what the child has to offer.

However, it is natural to ask questions, and some will be needed to ensure that the conversation is not incomprehensible. Questions are more successful if they relate to the theme of the conversation or to a contribution a child has already made.

Questions that begin with 'Where?' 'What?' 'Why?' 'When?' may help clarify a topic of conversation, as in the examples given below:

- Where did you go to play football?
- Where did you see the rabbit?
- What did you do after you put the flour in the bowl?
- What did you use to fix the broken toy car?
- Why did the doctor come to see your baby sister?
- Why do you need to look and listen when you cross the road?
- When did you fall over?
- When will you go to see grandma?

However, children will need to understand the concepts of time and place in order to answer questions beginning with 'When', 'What' or 'Where', and they will need to have a conceptual understanding of cause and effect before they can answer 'Why' or 'How' questions. Such questions are more likely to get an appropriate response if the children understand the relevance of the particular question word.

If a child does not respond to more general open questions, such as 'How do you feel today?' 'What did you do last week?' 'What would you like to play with?' or 'What do you want to drink?', then two-choice or forced-alternatives may be used. For example: 'Are you feeling happy or sad today?' 'Would you like milk or juice?' 'Do you want to play with the sand or the LEGO?'

Feedback

In order that children progress, it is necessary for them to know whether they have been successful in their attempts at communication. They need to know that they have understood what was said to them, that they have successfully conveyed their message and that their response has in turn been understood. Most of the time it is appropriate to tell them so, because it is important for them to know which of their efforts were successful so that they may repeat them in the future. This will help to build their confidence and inform them in a positive way about how they may continue to learn.

The natural way that adult listeners can indicate that the child's message has been successfully conveyed is by doing what is asked, or by continuing the conversation by expanding the topic being discussed. If children's messages are incomplete then an incorrect action or reply will let them know this.

Adults may help children to produce a clearer message by stating that their message was unclear, or seeking confirmation by asking them, 'Do you mean X or Y?' It is more difficult to communicate with a child whose speech is unintelligible as guesswork may be needed to aid interpretation.

If children fail to understand what they are being told or asked to do, then the message may need to be restated more simply. Requests may be repeated so that children have a second attempt at understanding what was said, or they may be broken down into simple stages, thereby reducing the length of the instruction which needs to be held in mind and understood at any one time. For example, 'Do you think you could see if there is a pair of scissors in the cupboard?' could be simplified to 'Please get the scissors. They are in the cupboard.'

As a last resort it may be possible to demonstrate the request. Altering what is said or increasing the amount of information in the instruction is likely to confuse more than assist the child.

How to monitor progress

In early years settings and as part of the Early Years Foundation Stage, keeping a record of developing skills and monitoring progress is an essential part of the work. It helps to identify where children have difficulties, whether they need help to make progress and whether any improvement is made following particular interventions by staff. Such record keeping is even more crucial when working with children with SLCN. The information will help to establish whether easier communication is a result of an improvement in the adult's ability to interpret the child's speech, or whether what the child says, and how s/he says it, has altered. These records also should highlight any change, particularly in children with multiple problems or behavioural difficulties, where progress may be slow or often not recognised. Without these records children whose behaviour has improved will not get that improvement recognised or recorded, particularly if their progress is slow.

The records used for children with SLCN can take the form of audio recordings, video recordings, checklists, or written records of children's understanding and use of language. The method selected will be influenced by the time available for the task. The information collected will enable the staff to know whether the language and activities selected for the children are pitched at an appropriate level and whether they are ready to progress to the next goal. Such information should be shared with parents on a regular basis, and many of the activities used in the early years settings can be carried out at home. Parents can also make notes to share with any professionals working with their child. It is assumed that the usual procedures for such recordings in any educational settings will be followed. That is, all recordings will be destroyed when the children are ready to leave the setting.

What language should be encouraged

Children with speech, language and communication problems mainly use language when they need help, for example with 'toileting' or feeding. Attempts at giving information and making social contact are often limited. Opportunities for using language in this way are more likely to occur in situations of significance to the child, such as discussion of current and home events or future outings. The content of the conversations will depend on the child's language skills. In an educational setting adults will usually take the lead in putting words to actions, introducing new vocabulary, or increasing the complexity of a child's utterances. The introduction of new materials needs to be controlled, so that there is recognisable order and progress can be noted. New words can be added to the child's vocabulary to help build on their existing skills.

Children with SLCN may need an environment that is organised and full of opportunities to hear and use language. Short, regular sessions during which language is specifically encouraged and responses are expected, and which build up the child's abilities gradually, are more likely to be successful and rewarding to both parties. This can be done in an early years setting or at home. Children are likely to tire quickly in tasks which require them to use their weaker skills, and after a while they may switch off or opt out.

Who should encourage language?

In order to give children the best chance of improving their communication skills, the social and physical environment need to be considered as well as the content of the interaction. Children with language difficulties are a varied group. Some may be quiet and withdrawn, while others are loud and difficult to manage.

Play provides children with the opportunity to understand their world, to work with others, and to use their language. As well as using their language during play children begin to link words with concepts and they begin to understand the world around them as they develop and demonstrate their understanding of the concepts of size, shape and colour. They also demonstrate during play their growth of symbolic understanding – the way in which children learn that miniature objects like toy cars can stand for life-sized ones, and that one object such as a building block can be used to represent something it does not at all resemble, such as a train. So a child can push the brick along the floor while making a noise like a train, showing everyone that the building block at that time is representing a train.

Children with communication problems may have difficulties starting and developing their play, which may often be repetitive and solitary. They may stand and watch other children playing together, but lack the skills required to begin a conversation and thereby become involved with another child. Limited play and language skills are likely to result in difficulties interacting with other children.

For children with SLCN, support and practise of their communication skills is unlikely to be provided by their peer group and they seldom use their language to form social contacts. Furthermore, they are less able to have successful and prolonged conversations with their classmates. Even children who do not have communication problems have a great deal of linguistic knowledge to acquire before they are as mature as adults in their communication. Even if they can engage well in a conversation with adults, they may not know how to initiate, continue or end a successful conversation with their peers. Thus they will possibly be unable, and probably unwilling, to facilitate a conversation with a child less able than themselves.

Children with language problems need the encouragement and the skills of the adults around them in order to help them develop their language. Initially the parent and/or early years worker may interact with the child on his/her own. As confidence and language skills increase, a child may be encouraged to play/work with one other child and then in a small group, before finally being expected to join in activities with larger groups of children. The adult's role in starting and maintaining the conversation can gradually be withdrawn.

The child with language difficulties often needs a great deal of individual attention and may find group situations difficult to handle. Even young children with normally developing speech and language find it no easy matter to make themselves understood in a group setting and to learn the rules of conversation such as seeking clarification or repairing conversations that go wrong. However, as Reilly (2012) shows, some small group activities may be useful for encouraging language.

Where should language be encouraged?

Conversations for young children are likely to revolve around the happenings and social practices of their everyday life. Although it may sometimes be necessary to withdraw children from the group for specific language work, wherever and whenever possible language should be encouraged during any group activities. This will ensure that the language used with the children is useful and meaningful.

It may be possible to arrange the environment in order to maximise the child's need to communicate and to make the meanings of words more apparent.

Maximising the child's need to communicate

For example, a wanted or needed object can be placed in a clear container with a lid which is difficult to remove, so that the child is more likely to request assistance. Alternatively, all the items required for a painting session, except the paint brushes, may be laid out. The children would then have to ask specifically for the brushes.

Making the meanings of words more apparent

For example, limit the number of options present in a similar way to the forced-alternative example given above. Ask, 'Do you want to paint flowers or play in the home corner?' In this example the adult has left out the three other activities the child could have become involved in because it was more helpful to limit the choice to one out of two activities. It may also be helpful to act on/do what the child has actually said to illustrate the meaning of the word that the child has used.

Many different opportunities can be provided to enable the child to discover the meanings of words and to use them in conversations. There are different situations where a word can occur – for example, the word 'in'.

This may appear in different contexts such as: the shopping is in the basket; the washing is in the machine; or the juice is in the cup. In these examples it is easy to demonstrate the 'shopping **in** the basket' and 'the washing **in** the machine and to ensure the children understand the use of the word 'in', since this is a 'natural' action. However, it may be possible to check the children's understanding of some words by asking them to follow unusual instructions and to do odd things. For example, 'Sit **under** the desk' or 'Crawl **under** the story mat'.

A shared interest is necessary for communication, so the content of the discussion must be mutually agreed upon. Initially this should be directed by the children's interest, by what they are looking at or playing with. An activity selected by the child is more likely to be maintained and is therefore the logical focus for conversation. Children will only really listen if you have their attention.

Different activities will influence the quantity and content of the language produced by the child. Construction tasks such as LEGO are unlikely to provide opportunities for extended conversations. Similarly, if the child is running around they will be out of breath and more concerned with action than with words.

Bruner (1980) found that fantasy play in the 'home corner' and play with dolls were more likely to encourage verbal exchanges. His seminal work also found that children said more in these environments when adults were not involved. However, as discussed earlier, children with speech, language and communication needs require the support of an adult in order to initiate and maintain the conversation.

Summary

Children with language problems are best helped by those who are interested in working with them. Positive improvement in a child's language development will be encouraged by parents and educational staff who are able to spend time with the child. They are in a position to provide the naturalistic setting in which children's language skills may develop. Although the children's progress may be gradual and continue throughout their time in education, with interest and enthusiasm from the staff combined with an understanding of language, the children may achieve their full potential.

References

Bruner, J.S. (1980) *Under Five in Britain*. Oxford: McIntyre Ltd.
Gross, J. (2013) *Time to Talk: Implementing outstanding practice in speech, language and communication*. London: Routledge.

Reilly, O. (2012) Managing Children Indivually or in Groups. In M. Kersner and J.A. Wright (Eds.) (2nd edition) *Speech and Language Therapy: The decision making process when working with children*. London: Routledge.

Further reading

Cooke, J. and Williams, D. (1997) *Working with Children's Language*. Bicester: Winslow Press/Speechmark. Edited by Claire Latham.
Delamain, C. and Spring, J. (2000) *Developing Baseline Communication Skills*. Bicester: Winslow Press/Speechmark.

Index